Critical Thinkers

Methods for Clear Thinking and Analysis in Everyday Situations
from the Greatest Thinkers in History

By Albert Rutherford
www.albertrutherford.com
albertrutherfordbooks@gmail.com

For general information on the products and services or to obtain technical support, please contact the author.

I have a gift for you…

Thank you for choosing my book, Practice Game Theory! I would like to show my appreciation for the trust you gave me by giving The Art of Asking Powerful Questions – in the World of Systems to you!

In this booklet you will learn:

-what bounded rationality is,

-how to distinguish event- and behavior-level analysis,

-how to find optimal leverage points,

-and how to ask powerful questions using a systems thinking perspective.

Visit www.albertrutherford.com to claim your gift: The Art of Asking Powerful Questions in the World of Systems

Written by Albert Rutherford
THE ART OF ASKING
POWERFUL QUESTIONS
IN THE WORLD OF SYSTEMS
FREE GIFT

Table of Contents

Chapter 1: Socrates and Aristotle

Socrates

Background.

Socrates is one of the most well-known Greek philosophers, and the earliest. His work focused on morals and were found solely in accounts written by his students, Plato and Xenophon; none of his own writing is known to exist.

He lived from roughly 470 BCE to 399 BCE and was a member of an aristocratic family. He began his career as a soldier, but eventually abandoned his family to become an itinerant teacher. His teachings, therefore, exist in the form of dialogue, rather than dense texts.[1]

The Socratic Method.

A teacher may have told you they were using the "Socratic method" during class discussions. This approach, developed by the philosopher Socrates and documented in his debates, involves a technique of intellectual inquiry.

[1] Kraut, Richard (2017). Socrates. Encyclopedia Britannica. Encyclopedia Britannica, Inc.

Socrates used this method to deconstruct his opponents' arguments to find the inevitable gaps in logic, contradictions, or lack of proof. He would ask his opponents a series of questions about their beliefs, eventually leading them to declare the flaws in their arguments.[2] You can think of this as the "question everything" mindset, which encourages people to question authority and preconceived beliefs or dogma.

Socrates's goal was to reveal that people in power are not necessarily always right. He believed that people should think for themselves and consider different arguments instead of blindly following their leaders.

This thinking process ideally involved gathering solid evidence, identifying flaws in logic, and predicting the consequences of actions and words. Clearly, the Socratic method is the most frequently used and famous critical thinking strategy because it provides a simple format for analyzing any argument.

Critical thinking shares the same goals as the Socratic method: analyzing beliefs and explanations, assessing what makes an argument reasonable, and distinguishing emotions from the intellectual merit of an argument or belief.

Socrates's student Plato, Plato's student Aristotle, and later Greek philosophers in the school of the skeptics, all developed this process of critical thinking to analyze the

---

[2] Paul, Richard. Elder, Linda. Bartell, Ted. (1997)A Brief History of the Idea of Critical Thinking. Critical Thinking. http://www.criticalthinking.org/pages/a-brief-history-of-the-idea-of-critical-thinking/408

appearance of things versus their true nature. Truth could be reached much faster without taking first impressions for granted, and instead thinking critically.

Critical thinking ultimately allows its practitioner to develop a more refined sense of personal reason. With well-developed judgment, a person can guide their thoughts, actions, and emotions more thoughtfully, rather than just going with gut reactions or pure emotion.

To provide a clearer understanding, the following outlines the five steps of the Socratic Method[3]:

1. **Initiate with a Hypothesis.**

The questioner starts by asking for a clear hypothesis from the interlocutor. If the hypothesis is unclear, the questioner may rephrase the question or suggest alternatives.

2. **Examine the Hypothesis.**

Once a clear hypothesis is provided, the questioner begins to examine it by asking for evidence, reasoning, counterexamples, or alternative perspectives.

3. **Response and Revision.**

---

[3] Winter, T. (2017). Smarter thinking: The Socratic method. HPT by DTS. https://blog.hptbydts.com/smarter-thinking-the-socratic-method

The interlocutor responds to the examination, which may involve agreeing, disagreeing, clarifying, or revising their hypothesis based on the discussion.

4. **Further Examination.**

The questioner may continue to probe different aspects of the reasoning, guide the interlocutor towards alternative views, or address new responses as the dialogue progresses.

5. **Dialogue and Conclusion.**

The dialogue continues with a back-and-forth exchange that can last from a few seconds to several hours. It may end with a revised hypothesis or the same hypothesis after thorough examination, depending on the nature of the discussion and the participants' engagement.

Now, it's important to understand that the Socratic method is nothing without asking questions. The essence of this method lies in the art of Socratic questioning—constantly probing, challenging, and examining the validity of arguments.

Socratic Questioning.[4]

Socratic questioning is a simple and easy way to develop critical thinking skills because it allows the

---

[4] Paul, R. and Elder, L. (1997). Socratic Teaching. Foundation For Critical Thinking. http://www.criticalthinking.org/pages/socratic-teaching/606

practitioner to quite literally examine any flaws within an argument.

There's no limitation to the types of questions one can ask in the Socratic method, but some questions are more helpful to the critical thinking process than others. Questions should be focused, respectful, intellectual, and critical; tuned to analyze processes, ask for more data, brainstorm interpretations, and counter assumptions.

A Socratic questioner should be comfortable asking questions that keep the conversation moving, "moderate" the discussion, summarizing occasionally to recap what has been said, and making sure everyone is included and able to speak.

Below are six types of Socratic questions[5] along with examples[6]:

1. **Clarification questions.**

These help you understand the context behind someone's response and ensure you have a clearer grasp of their meaning. For example, if a colleague says, "I think we should change our approach," you could ask, "Could you elaborate on what you mean by changing our approach?" or "How do you see this fitting into our current agenda?"

---

[5] Kwantlen Polytechnic University. (2018) Critical Thinking through Socratic Questioning. https://www.kpu.ca/sites/default/files/Learning%20Centres/Think_Critical_LA.pdf

[6] Paul, R. (1993). Critical thinking: What Every Person Needs to Survive in a Rapidly Changing World. Sonoma State University, Center for Critical Thinking & Moral Critique. https://www.criticalthinking.org/data/pages/79/770a28b6dfcc0886bbeca1dd1195a2bf51363f3ba852c.pdf

Other examples:

- "Can you help me understand why…?"
- "Could you clarify what you mean by…?"
- "How does this connect with our conversation?"

2. **Assumption questions.**

These challenge the basic assumptions behind a statement or argument to see if they are valid. They help you figure out if the underlying beliefs make sense and are backed by solid evidence. Let's say someone says, "Investing in this stock is the best way to make a lot of money." Assumption questions sound like, "What makes you think this stock is the best money-maker?" or "How can we check if your assumption about that stock is accurate or not?"

Other examples:

- What are other assumptions we can consider?
- How can we verify if this assumption is accurate or not?
- What's your reasoning behind…?

3. **Perspective questions.**

These explore different perspectives and understand how other viewpoints might influence the discussion. They help strengthen the conversation by considering alternative angles. For instance, imagine you and your partner are discussing moving to a bigger house. You can ask a perspective question by saying, "What are the pros and cons of moving to a bigger house?"

Other examples:

- What other options do we have?
- How are X and Y's idea alike? How are they different?
- What makes X the best choice?

4. **Reason/evidence questions.**

These uncover the reasons and evidence behind an argument or explanations for a phenomenon. Let's say you bump into a salesman promoting a car, claiming it's the best in the market. In response, you can ask, "Do you have evidence to prove that?" or "What are the reasons or features that make this car stand out from others?"

Other examples:

- Can you provide evidence that supports this conclusion?
- What other information do I need?
- What do you think causes this to happen?

5. **Consequence questions.**

These focus on figuring out the potential outcomes of a decision. They encourage thinking about how a particular choice might impact other areas or lead to specific results.

Consequence questions can work well during announcements of a policy change.

For example, your boss might announce, “We're implementing a new remote work policy starting next month. Do you have any questions?” You can raise your hand to ask, “What could be the impact of this new policy on productivity?” or “How does this affect the company culture?”

Other examples:

- What are you implying?
- What effect would that have?
- If that happened, what would be the consequences?

6. **Meta-questions.**

These ask the purpose behind a question or its relevance to the conversation. They also encourage the person asking to reflect on the process of their inquiry and consider whether they’re truly asking the right question. These can be handy when the current questions being brought up are leading to unproductive discussions. For instance, you can ask, “What’s the point of that question?” or “Can we break down that question?”

Other examples:

- Do you agree that you’re asking the right question?

- Why are you asking this?
- How does that question improve our discussion?

Exercise.

Using what you've learned, form Socratic questions in response to the given statement. Here's an example:

Statement: "Social media platforms are harmful to mental health."

1. **Clarifying Question:** "What specific aspects of social media are considered harmful to mental health?"
2. **Assumption Question:** "What assumptions are we making about the relationship between social media use and mental health issues?
3. **Reason/evidence Question:** "What evidence exists that social media use contributes to mental health problems?"
4. **Perspective Question:** "How might different age groups experience the impact of social media on their mental health?"
5. **Consequence Questions:** "What are the potential societal implications if social media is proven to have a harmful effect on mental health?
6. **Meta-question:** "Why is it crucial to understand the impact of social media on mental health?

Now it's your turn! Create Socratic questions based on the provided statement below.

Statement: "Technology is making students more distracted in the classroom."

1. Clarifying Question:

   ____

2. Assumption Question:

   ____

3. Perspective Question:

   ____

4. Reason/evidence Question:

   ____

5. Consequence Question:

   ____

6. Meta-Question:

   ____

Elements of Thought.

Richard Paul and Linda Elder, the modern critical thinking theorists, developed a paradigm called the Elements of Thought, an intrinsic part of their critical thinking framework.

They have interwoven the Socratic method into this framework as well because it is important to overall critical thinking. The questions act as a stimulant for the brain's creative and analytic processes. This is because each known piece of information can be found using a question.

Therefore, asking the right questions—that is, the ones given in the Socratic format—can help students parse out inconsistencies in others' arguments, flaws in reasoning, and creative solutions to problems. This is what critical thinking is all about.

While the Elements of Thought vary from the Socratic method, it is are based in the foundations of Socrates's thinking process. They involve thinking about the origins of thoughts, and the questions to ask based on these backgrounds.

Aside from that, they also explore why someone holds their particular beliefs, understand the assumptions behind their views, or consider the potential outcomes of a specific thought. In short, Paul and Elder's critical thinking types align well with the questions in the Socratic method.

Every statement in a textbook is an answer to a question, but we never think about textbooks this way. Why? Because teachers often like to teach as much material as possible, as opposed to training students to thoughtfully engage with the things they learn. This divorces answers from questions, because only answers are given, but in fact, anything you could possibly learn is the answer to a question.

If your teacher says the primary habitat of a lion is the savanna, they're also indirectly asking you where the lions live. And that information can be translated into a focused Socratic question by asking, "Why is the savanna the primary habitat of lions?"

We improve our thinking not with the answers we're given, but with the questions we ask. For example, if Newton hadn't wondered why things fall, we might have never discovered gravity. Questions drive us to make crucial developments in a variety of fields. They're at the heart of all human knowledge–without questions, there would be no answers.

Paul and Elder give a longer list of critically oriented questions than Socrates does, but theirs also focus on probing the questions behind life's common answers.

- Questioning the purpose of your task can help you decide its intentionality.
- Asking yourself where your information comes from can help you interrogate its quality and factuality, as can thinking about whether information is accurate.
- Reflecting on the perspective behind an 'answer' can help you interpret it through the lens of its source.
- Asking yourself, "How is something logically argued?" is one of the important questions you can consider.

- Examining the logical process behind your conclusion can help clarify how you arrived at it.

In the end, interrogating yourself with these kinds of questions will make you a sharper critical thinker. Without these or similar questions, your understanding of any given issue will be shallow and limited. Although it's difficult to ask intellectual questions regularly, doing so can help you find deeper answers and purpose in your own life.[7]

[7] Critical Thinking. (2018) The Role of Socratic Questioning in Thinking, Teaching, and Learning. http://www.criticalthinking.org/pages/the-role-of-socratic-questioning-in-thinking-teaching-amp-learning/522

Aristotle

Background.

Aristotle lived from 384 BCE to 322 BCE, so he didn't know Socrates in his lifetime. However, like Socrates, he was a highly accomplished Greek philosopher and is still credited as one of the founders of Western philosophy which uses many Aristotelean methods and terms in modern work. His work laid the groundwork for many principles still used in modern science. In terms of influence, Aristotle is at least on par with Socrates, if not more so.

Aristotle's inclination for critical thinking is reflected in his works, especially the *Metaphysics*, which he wrote in roughly 350 BCE. In it, he argued that every person has a thirst for knowledge, that humans are interested in learning and knowing things for the sake of knowing. This observation began the philosophical practice of a divided field, focusing either on exploring deep questions -called philosophical or abstract thinking- or thinking that has a real-world effect in improving humans' lives, which is the core for critical thinking.

Aristotle remains highly influential in current critical thinking models and practices. His emphasis on linguistic precision and careful word choice is still valued today. Critical thinking necessitates being able to articulate ideas carefully and accurately. Definitions, for example, should be organized into the *genus (a broad category)* and the *diaphora (a specific characteristic).* This is something practitioners have valued since Aristotle's time.[8]

Take your car, for example. In the *genus*, or broad category, it's a land vehicle. Now, try to categorize the car into its “species.” Is it gas or electric-powered, and can it be operated independently by the driver to move small groups of people? When you combine these two categories, you can define a car as a land vehicle that is powered by fuel, operated independently, and carries small groups of people.

This system of categorization helps you clearly and concisely describe the car, making it easier to evaluate whether it's the right transportation for your needs. The *diaphora* helps to distinguish the car from the other things that could be in its broader categories.

You can also refer to the specific categories as differentia. Combining these categories gives a descriptive definition of your car. This can be done for anything to come up with a critically reasoned definition of what that concept or thing is, allowing you to perform further critical thinking.

Syllogisms.[9]

---

[8] Stratton, Jon. (1999) Critical Thinking for College Students. Rowman & Littlefield Publishers. ISBN-10: 0847696022.

[9] Smith, Robin, “Aristotle's Logic”, The Stanford Encyclopedia of Philosophy (Winter 2018 Edition), Edward N. Zalta. https://plato.stanford.edu/entries/aristotle-logic/#AriLogWorOrg

Aristotle practiced deductive logic, or deduction. You might have heard this term used by Sherlock Holmes— it's a very effective mode of critical thinking.

Deductive logic is the process of reasoning from one or more statements to reach a logically correct conclusion. Deductive logic labels the statements in your argument the "premises", such as the principle of gravity, or that your car gets good gas mileage (if you're contending that the car we've defined is a good car).

The conclusion is what you are trying to prove, i.e., that you own a good car. The logic behind this is that your conclusion has to result from your premiscs if your conclusion could not be false when your premises are true. This method is commonly used to assess whether an argument is "valid," or logically consistent, in philosophical inquiry.

Exercise.

Use deductive logic to determine if a specific car is a good car based on given premises.

Step 1: Identify the Premises

Write down the premises that will be used to form your conclusion.

Premise 1: All cars with excellent gas mileage are considered good cars.

Write your version here:

____

Premise 2: This car has excellent gas mileage.

Write your version here:

____

Step 2: Formulate the Conclusion

Based on the premises, write down the conclusion you are trying to prove.

Conclusion: _______________________________

Step 3: Logical Connection

Check if the conclusion logically follows from the premises.

Premise 1: All cars with excellent gas mileage are considered good cars.
Premise 2: This car has excellent gas mileage.
Question: Does the conclusion logically follow from the premises? Explain why or why not.

Your explanation: ________________________________

Step 4: Validate the Argument

Determine if the argument is valid. For an argument to be valid, the conclusion must be true if the premises are true.

Premise 1: True or False?
Premise 2: True or False?

Question: If both premises are true, is the conclusion necessarily true?
Your answer: ______________________________

Step 5: Reflection

Reflect on the deductive logic process used in this exercise.

- What did you learn about forming valid conclusions?

Your reflection: ______________________________

The process of deduction gets you from your premises to your conclusion by testing whether true premises lead to a true conclusion. It's a practical method of critical thinking. When you use this approach to prove something—like saying your car is good because it has low gas mileage—you've got a syllogism. That's where a big premise and more specific premise lead logically to a conclusion.

Example:

Premise 1: All cars with excellent gas mileage are considered good cars.

Premise 2: This car has excellent gas mileage.
Conclusion: Therefore, this car is a good car.

Syllogism: This argument is a syllogism because it combines a general premise with a specific premise to reach a logical conclusion.

Logical Connection: The conclusion follows logically because if all cars with excellent gas mileage are good, and this car has excellent gas mileage, then this car must be good.

Validation: If both premises are true, the conclusion must be true, so the argument is valid.

Identify Premise Types.

Premises in syllogisms can be:

- "All ___ are ___" (Universal)
- "Some ___ are ___" (Particular)
- "Some ___ are not ___" (Particular)
- "No ___ are ___" (Universal)

Identify whether the following premises are universal or particular:

1. All mammals are warm-blooded.
2. Some mammals are marine animals.
3. No birds are mammals.

Your answers:

1.

2.

3.

Modern formal logic allows more possibilities for premises' forms, but this chapter won't get into that. [10]

Each premise must relate to the conclusion through a specific term; in our above example, the big premise relates to the conclusion through "good cars," while the specific premise relates to the conclusion through "your car."

The big premise relates through the conclusion's predicating condition, while the minor term relates through the subject of the conclusion. Therefore, "good cars" is the major term and "your car" is the minor term, while the middle term is "good gas mileage." If both premises are universal; meaning they apply to all cases the conclusion is also universal.

Aristotle remains highly influential, and his way of thinking has fundamentally shaped academia profoundly, impacting scholarship, science, and religion during the Middle Ages and the Renaissance. His work continues to guide academic philosophy and practical ethics today.

Reflect on Socratic and Aristotelian Wisdom.

---

[10] Michael Frede, "Stoic vs. Peripatetic Syllogistic", Archive for the History of Philosophy 56, 1975, 99-124.

As we close this chapter on Socrates and Aristotle, take a moment to reflect on what you've learned. Answer the questions below to deepen your understanding:

1. How do Socrates' and Aristotle's philosophies compare in terms of their approach to understanding the world and personal development?

2. What insights from their teachings can you apply to your current goals or areas where you seek improvement?

3. How can adopting the Socratic method in your daily conversations and decision-making processes help you challenge your own assumptions and improve your critical thinking skills?

4. In what situations might deductive reasoning be particularly useful, and how can you apply it effectively in those contexts?

Chapter 2: Thomas Aquinas

Background.

Thomas Aquinas, now a saint in the Roman Catholic Church, was born in 1225 in Italy and died 1274, living at the height of the 13th century's flourishing academic culture. A well-educated Dominican friar, he became a leading philosopher and Christian theologian of the medieval era.

Deeply involved in the university culture of his time, he was a key figure in classical natural theology and scholasticism.[11] He eventually founded his own school of philosophy and theology, called Thomism. Thomism is centered on the idea that reason is found in God. Aquinas's writings on the reasoning behind Christian doctrine and theology are still widely circulated and contributed to his sainthood.

Aquinas' ideas also proved to be an enduring lightning rod for philosophy, with many lasting ideas and debates in modern philosophy stemming from arguments about his ideas regarding ethics, metaphysics, political theory, and the idea of natural law. He was heavily

---

[11] Scholasticism was a popular pedagogical school in medieval Europe rooted in the idea of disputation as a method for cultivating rigorous critical thought. It reached its height in Aquinas's era, which coincided with the development of the modern university as instructional institutions for the clergy.

influenced by Aristotle, and much of his work is a synthesis of Aristotelean philosophy and Christian doctrine. His most famous works, *Summa Theologica* and *Summa Contra Gentiles*, are classic examples of his effort to use logic to explain and defend Christian religious beliefs.[12]

Aquinas held empiricist beliefs that the truth is objective and discoverable, either through natural revelation made available to all people who could use their reason to discover it, or through supernatural revelation found in scripture or visions. He did not see these two types of revelation as oppositional beliefs; instead, he believed they coexisted, and people could use critical thinking and reasoning on both.

He is honored as a Doctor of the Church and serves as the patron saint of scholars, schools, and students. Nearly 800 years after his death, his legacy still impacts how we understand truth, learning, and faith. Dominican Sister of Hope Diane Trotta, O.P., reflects, "As a young adult, Saint Thomas Aquinas helped shape my spirituality, study, and my nursing ministry."[13]

---

[12] Philosophy Basics. (2018) St. Thomas Aquinas. Philosophy Basics. https://www.philosophybasics.com/philosophers_aquinas.html

[13] Ciliberto, G.(2019, January 28) 4 Practices of Saint Thomas Aquinas that Influence Us Today .Dominican Sisters of Hope. https://ophope.org/spirituality/saint-thomas-aquinas-feast-day-dominican-order/ Sayles,N.(2013)

Aquinas's Contributions to Critical Thinking.

Aquinas's chief logical strategy in his writings was to consider all possible counterarguments to his ideas and address them within the text. This way he would arrive at the most critically well-reasoned conclusion possible.

His key innovation in the field of critical thinking is akin to modern courtroom cross-examination. This innovation also allowed room for the interrogation of the logic and roots of beliefs without the rejection of the belief itself, which makes it decidedly different from the Socratic or Aristotelean methods. Unlike older Greek methods, which would dismiss an answer if it wasn't logically sound, Aquinas focused on scrutinizing the thought *process* rather than discarding the thought.

Applying Aquinas's Critical Thinking Method.

Learn to apply Thomas Aquinas's method for evaluating arguments by addressing counterarguments and refining your reasoning.

1. State Your Main Argument.

Question: What is the main argument or thesis you want to evaluate?

Example Answer: "Eating a balanced diet improves overall health."

Your Answer:

___

2. Identify Possible Counterarguments.

Question: What are some possible objections or counterarguments to your main argument?

Counterargument 1: "A balanced diet can be expensive and not affordable for everyone."

Your Counterargument 2:

___

3. Address Each Counterargument.

Question: How would you respond to each counterargument to strengthen your argument?

Response to Counterargument 1: Healthy eating can be budget-friendly with careful planning and choosing cost-effective, nutritious foods. There are also community resources and programs to help with food affordability.

Your Response to Counterargument 2:

___

___

____

____

4. Review the Logic and Foundations.

Question: Does the logic behind your main argument hold up when examined closely? What evidence supports your argument?

____

____

____

____

Logic Check: Does the argument that a balanced diet improves health make sense based on evidence and common knowledge?

____

Foundations: Consider why eating a balanced diet is important. What benefits to health are supported by research or personal experience?

a.)

b.)

c.)

5. Refine Your Argument

Question: Based on the responses to counterarguments and the review of logic, how would you refine your argument to address any weaknesses?

____

____

____

____

____

Refined Argument: "Eating a balanced diet improves overall health. Although it can be costly and time-consuming, planning and making use of available resources can make it more accessible. The benefits of a balanced diet, supported by health research, outweigh these challenges."

6. Reflect on Your Process.

Question 1: How did addressing counterarguments help strengthen your argument?

____

____

____

____

____

Question 2: Did examining the logic and foundations provide a clearer understanding of the argument's validity?

____

Reflection: Reflect on how considering objections and refining your argument improved its overall strength and clarity.

____
____
____
____

Aquinas used a very specific literary device to interrogate his own ideas. He wrote his works in the style of a scholastic disputation, as one would find in the universities of Italy or France during the period. This meant he would have a debate with himself, identifying and addressing weaknesses in his arguments point by point until he reached a well-reasoned conclusion. This would make his arguments stronger, which was crucial given that any evidence against Christian doctrine would not be acceptable. His critical thinking method reflects the academic practices of his era and remains relevant today. Disputation is still used in classrooms today to encourage students to think more carefully about the flaws in their arguments and is widely recognized as a useful pedagogical tool.[14]

Scholastic Disputation in Aquinas's Writing.

Understand how Aquinas used scholastic disputation to test and strengthen his ideas.

[14] Careful Nursing. (2015) Critical Thinking: Guidelines from Thomas Aquinas. http://www.carefulnursing.ie/go/blog/2015-05/critical-thinking-guidelines-from-thomas-aquinas

Step 1: Understand Scholastic Disputation.

Scholastic disputation involves a method where the writer debates with themselves, identifying and addressing weaknesses in their arguments to reach a solid conclusion.

Question: Describe how Aquinas used scholastic disputation to refine his arguments.

Your answer:

Step 2: Example of Scholastic Disputation.

In scholastic disputation, a writer would outline their main argument, then list potential objections or weaknesses and respond to each one.

Example: If Aquinas were arguing that his homemade apple pie is the best dessert, he would:

1. State why the pie is the best (e.g., "It has the perfect balance of sweetness and tartness").
2. List possible objections (e.g., "But is the crust really as flaky as it should be?").
3. Address each objection (e.g., "Yes, because I use a special recipe for the crust").

Question: Create your own example where you use scholastic disputation to argue for a position (e.g., why a particular method is the best for managing tasks).

Your example:

Step 3: Apply the Method.

Use scholastic disputation to examine an argument or claim of your choice. List the main argument, potential objections, and responses.

Main Argument:

Objection 1:

Response to Objection 1:

Objection 2:

Response to Objection 2:

Conclusion:

Step 4: Reflect on the Process.

Reflect on how the process of disputation helped clarify and strengthen your argument.

Question: How did using scholastic disputation improve your understanding of the argument?

Your reflection:

Use this exercise to practice the method of scholastic disputation and see how it helps in refining and strengthening your arguments.

Aquinas's Ideas.

Free Will.

Aquinas didn't just defend free will because scripture said so—like in Sirach 15:14, "He himself made man from the beginning, and left him in the hand of his counsel"—he also understood that free will has real consequences for how we live, how society functions, and how we understand right from wrong.

In his Disputations on the Question of Evil, Aquinas addressed the challenge of free will in the context of divine control. Some argued that if God is in charge of all actions, humans don't have real free will. Aquinas disagreed, explaining that not all compulsion is the same. He argued that true moral judgment requires actions to come from within us, not be imposed from outside forces.

According to Aquinas, without free will, the whole concept of ethics falls apart. Without free will, there's no point in talking about moral responsibility, justice, or even the dignity of human choice. His stance on free will helps maintain the moral framework and supports the fairness of divine judgment.[15]

Diversity.

Aquinas had a sensible take on cultural diversity, which is especially relevant in today's world where ethical issues often come up. He viewed cultural differences as part of the world's natural order, not something to be eliminated. According to Aquinas, addressing these differences means balancing universal moral principles with the specific contexts of different cultures.

He focused on practical wisdom, neighborly love, and natural moral law, guiding people to respect cultural diversity while sticking to core ethical values. Aquinas's approach isn't about rigid, one-size-fits-all rules, or moral relativism. Instead, it's about finding a middle ground that allows for meaningful dialogue and respect for diverse perspectives while maintaining a foundation of universal principles. His ideas offer a practical way to handle diversity

---

[15] Krasue, P. (2019, July 19). Aquinas on free will, sin, and ethics. https://minervawisdom.com/2019/07/19/aquinas-on-free-will-sin-and-ethics/#_ftn2

by integrating both broad ethical standards and cultural specifics.[16]

Narrow-Mindedness.

Aquinas also believed that narrow-mindedness is bad because it limits perspective and hampers well-reasoned decisions. Being able to see others' perspectives is vital to critical thinking, and its importance cannot be discounted. Open-mindedness is still valued at universities, other academic institutions, and in the world at large.

Equality.

Aquinas wrote "all men are equal in liberty, but not in other endowments." This reflects a belief in the basic right to liberty for everyone, though it must be understood in the context of medieval society. Of course, it is a matter of interpretation as to whether this includes women or people from other parts of the world other than where Aquinas lived.

Risk.

Aquinas seemed to believe that a certain amount of risk, whether it be intellectual, spiritual, or any other kind, was necessary to success in any endeavor. Important ideas require risk-taking, as does critical thinking. Reflect on the

---

[16] das Neves, J.C., Melé, D. Managing Ethically Cultural Diversity: Learning from Thomas Aquinas. J Bus Ethics 116, 769–780 (2013). https://doi.org/10.1007/s10551-013-1820-1

risks you might take in critically evaluating and questioning your own ideas. While these risks might seem daunting, they pale in comparison to the valuable insights you could gain about yourself and the world.

Independent Thought.

Aquinas also held that true living involves independent thought and action. If others are running your life, you're not really living. This is also an argument for critical thinking because a crucial step in successful critical thinking is being able to keep others from influencing your argument. Try to keep other people's voices out of your head when puzzling out your ideas. You'll feel much freer to consider other options and answers to the questions you have.

Faith and Reason.

Aquinas viewed both faith and reason as fundamental to achieving true understanding of the world, and of God. Following Aristotle, he believed truth was revealed through the study of nature, but he also believed God was revealed through nature, therefore fusing Aristotle with Christian ideas.

In his *Summa Theologica*, Aquinas presented five logical arguments for the existence of God, known as The Five Ways:

- **The Argument of the Unmoved Mover**: This argument declares everything that moves needs a mover, so there needs to be a mover who doesn't move at the bottom of everything in the universe. This "prime mover," as the concept is known in Platonic philosophy as God.
- **The Argument of the First Cause**: Every effect has a cause, and every cause has another cause. There must be a first cause that isn't caused by anything else, which Aquinas identifies as God.
- **The Argument from Contingency:** Everything that exists is contingent on the existence of something else. However, there needs to be something not contingent on another thing to cause this chain, and this must be God. This can be thought of as the solution to the chicken-and-the-egg problem.
- **The Argument from Degree:** Since some things in the universe are more perfect than others, there must be a hierarchy of perfection. At the top of this hierarchy there needs to be something that is the most perfect. This is God.
- **The Argument from Design:** (Also known as the teleological argument.) All natural bodies work towards specific ends, which

implies intelligence guiding them. This intelligent being is God.

The Five Ways are landmark pieces of theology as they try to explain God rationally. Before Aquinas, people tended to think of Christianity in more doctrinal terms, with unquestioning belief in Scripture being the primary mode of theology and spirituality. Aquinas stands out because he took the university approach of teaching the liberal arts and applied it to Christian theology. This was a bold move, as challenging traditional beliefs could be seen as heretical.[17]

Practical Application of Thomistic Disputation.

The disputation works well as a critical thinking strategy precisely because it requires the thinker to consider and successfully reject every possible argument against the thinker's idea. If all counterarguments are rejected, the argument is good, but if a counterargument can't be rejected the thinker must reconsider the original idea.

This approach has stuck around because it's a solid way to test ideas. Whether you're tackling a research question in literature or science, the process of introducing and refuting counterarguments is key. If you can't dismiss them, either revise your hypothesis or propose a new model for others to explore. In other words, disputation's principles have lasted because they rigorously test an idea's validity.

[17] Aquinas, Thomas. (1981) Summa Theologica. Christian Classics.

Beyond the academic realm, disputation is handy in everyday critical thinking. It requires the thinker to assess what they already know about a topic, set aside personal biases, and carefully examine it. If you think about all the possible counterarguments to whatever argument you want to make and preemptively refute them, your own argument will be much stronger. For example, you want to argue that your car is a good one, apply disputation like this:

- Your thought: "My car is a good car." To set up a dispute, ask yourself, "Is my car a good car?"
- **Anticipate Counterarguments:** Consider objections why your car is not a good car, like:
  a.) "Your car is old and has many miles."
  b.) "It's small and not safe for highway driving."
  c.) "It lacks a car charger."
  d.) "The headlights are manual, which might lead to forgetting them."
- Refute the Counterarguments: Develop responses that would support why your car is a good car, such as:

a.) "My car might have a lot of miles, but I haven't had to make any serious repairs."

b.) "My car is small, but it gets thirty miles per gallon so it's cheap to get gas. Plus, I don't need to drive on the highway."

c.) "I don't need a car charger, I can bring a mobile battery pack wherever I go."

d.) "The car beeps after I turn it off until I turn my headlights off, so I won't forget to turn them off."

If the counterarguments don't seem sufficient, either revisit the validity of your idea based on universal standards or see if you could make your counterarguments stronger. Now you're critically thinking about your ideas and beliefs.[18]

Evaluate a Decision to Take a New Job

You're considering whether to accept a new job offer. Your initial thought is that this new position could be a great move for your career.

1. **State Your Claim.**

Start by clearly stating your initial claim about the job offer.

Write Your Claim: "Taking this new job is a good decision for my career."

2. **Frame your Claim as a Question.**

Turn your claim into a question to set up the disputation.

Formulate the Question: "Is taking this new job a good decision for my career?"

3. **Identifying Counterarguments, Anticipate Objections.**

---

[18] Careful Nursing. (2015) Critical Thinking: Guidelines from Thomas Aquinas. http://www.carefulnursing.ie/go/blog/2015-05/critical-thinking-guidelines-from-thomas-aquinas

Think of potential objections or concerns about taking the new job.

List Counterarguments:

1. "The new job has a longer commute, which could affect my work-life balance."
2. "The salary increase might not be as significant as expected after taxes and benefits are considered."

3. ....
4. ....
5. ....

4. Developing Refutations, Address Each Counterargument.

Refute each counterargument to support your original claim.

1. "Although the commute is longer, the flexibility of remote workdays compensates for this."
2. "The salary increase is modest, but the job offers better long-term growth opportunities."

3. ....
4. ....
5.

5.Evaluate Your Argument.

Review whether your initial claim still stands after addressing counterarguments.

- Does your argument that taking the new job is a good decision still hold strong? [Yes/No]
- If not, what changes or additional factors should you consider? [Write your thoughts here]

    1.
    2.
    3.

6. **Reflection.**

   Think about how the disputation process helped you better understand the decision.

7. Write a Reflection:

How did considering and refuting counterarguments impact your view of the job offer?

____

____

8. Apply Disputation to Other Situations.

Identify other decisions or opinions where you can use this method.

Identify New Areas:

- In what other situations can you apply this disputation method to make better decisions or form stronger arguments?

____

____

Great job working through this activity! The disputation method isn't just a historical curiosity; it's a practical tool for critical thinking that remains relevant today. By rigorously testing your ideas against counterarguments, you're building stronger, more thoughtful arguments and making better decisions.

This approach, inspired by Thomas Aquinas, underpins much of modern critical thinking and helps us blend diverse perspectives into clearer, more reasoned conclusions. Keep using this method to refine your ideas and decisions in all areas of your life.

Chapter 3: Sir Francis Bacon

> "I found that I was fitted for nothing so well as for the study of Truth; as having a mind nimble and versatile enough to catch the resemblances of things (which is the chief point), and at the same time steady enough to fix and distinguish their subtler differences; as being gifted by nature with the desire to seek, patience to doubt, fondness to meditate, slowness to assert, readiness to consider, carefulness to dispose and set in order; and hatred for every kind of imposture."
>
> -Francis Bacon, 1605

Background.

Francis Bacon, born in England in 1561 and died in 1626, lived through the later Renaissance, during the peak of its spread from Italy into northern Europe. He was interested in many Renaissance ideas, particularly the role of the mind in the pursuit of knowledge. He believed the mind needed disciplined training to effectively pursue knowledge, rather than being left to figure things out on its own.

In his book *The Advancement of Learning,* Bacon emphasized that it was important to study the world with an empirical eye. Much like a modern scientist, he was focused on gathering objective information. He also recognized that people developed bad thinking habits when their minds weren't properly trained. He referred to these bad habits as "idols" which I will present in detail later in this chapter.

But what makes Francis Bacon significant today is his major contribution to the school of empiricism. Interestingly, he believed that the best way to acquire scientific knowledge was to observe phenomena and use inductive reasoning.[19]

Bacon also believed that people were naturally prone to deceiving themselves about their work. He argued for the most objective and skeptical perspective possible. Even though his own method didn't endure, his ideas about the scientific process eventually led to the foundation of the scientific method. His revolutionary approaches to scientific theory continue to influence and shape academic discussions on scientific methodology.

Francis Bacon and Critical Thinking.

One of Bacon's key innovations was to move scholarly culture away from absolute reverence for "traditional" scholarly methods.

---

[19] Empiricism emphasizes observable evidence over logical reasoning and traditional thought, unless traditions are based on observed evidence. This is very different from Aristotle, who emphasized reasoning; instead, here real-life experience is the best teacher.

These were found in European universities and derived from Greek philosophers such as Plato and Aristotle, as well as old theological texts. Bacon believed that old ideas about how the mind and knowledge should work were outdated, and that to achieve objective truth one had to hold minimal assumptions before investigating a problem.

Bacon is frequently cited as "the Father of Induction" because this way of thinking was so new, and fundamentally changed critical thinking. He believed in experiments instead of Aristotle's theoretical framework, which is why he's often viewed as a transitional figure between the Renaissance and the Early Modern period.

Another of Bacon's crucial insights was that the human brain doesn't always reason perfectly. To begin a scientific experiment, one must set aside personal ideas, goals, and biases. He, therefore, understood concepts like confirmation bias due to his deep understanding of human nature and brain functions.

Idols of The Mind.

In *Novum Organum,* Francis Bacon described the flaws of the mind in very modern terms:

> "The mind, hastily and without choice, imbibes and treasures up the first notices of *things, from whence all the rest proceed, errors must forever prevail, and remain uncorrected.*

[...]

The human understanding when it has once adopted an opinion (either as being the received opinion or as being agreeable to itself) draws all things else to support and agree with it. And though there be a greater number and weight of instances to be found on the other side, yet these it either neglects and despises, or else by some distinction sets aside and rejects, in order that by this great and pernicious predetermination the authority of its former conclusions may remain inviolate."

Bacon believed that bad thinking habits often manifest in how we delude ourselves, misuse language, get trapped in mental ruts, and blindly follow authority. These flaws in human thinking were what he famously identified as "Idols of the Mind".

In his understanding, there were four main types of idols: *Idols of the Tribe, Idols of the Theater, Idols of the Cave, and Idols of the Marketplace.*[20]

Idols of The Tribe.

In ancient Greece, Hippocrates, the father of medicine, proposed that bad air, or "miasma,"[21] was the cause of diseases. Rejecting supernatural explanations, he

---

[20] Farnam Street. (2018) Francis Bacon and the Four Idols of the Mind. https://fs.blog/2016/05/francis-bacon-four-idols-mind/

[21] Kannadan, Ajesh (2018) "History of the Miasma Theory of Disease," ESSAI: Vol. 16 , Article 18. Available at: https://dc.cod.edu/essai/vol16/iss1/18

suggested that foul air from decaying matter made people sick. This intuitive idea led to improvements in air quality being seen as a cure for illness.

The belief persisted through the ages. During the Middle Ages, physicians like Galen expanded on Hippocrates' theory, which influenced medical practices and public health policies. For example, the British Parliament passed laws to prevent waste from contaminating waterways, aiming to avoid corrupting the air.

In the 14th century, Spanish-Arab physician Ibn Khatimah supported this view, arguing that foul-smelling air was directly responsible for disease outbreaks. The name "malaria" itself reflects this belief, with "mala aria" meaning "bad air" in Italian.

This reliance on sensory impressions—foul smells suggesting harmful air—illustrates Idols of the Tribe.

Basically, this idol is linked to the idea that trusting natural impressions without solid evidence can falsify our understanding of the nature of things, leading to oversimplified and incorrect theories, such as the miasma theory, which was eventually debunked.

Idols of The Cave.

Marie Antoinette[22], born an Austrian archduchess on November 2, 1755, entered the grandeur of Versailles at just

14 as the wife of King Louis XVI. Raised in a world of luxury, she found herself in an even more opulent setting as Queen of France, far removed from the daily struggles of ordinary French people.

Her life quickly became a series of extravagant parties, hundreds of gowns, and costly renovations to her private retreat, Petit Trianon. While her passion for fashion and beauty was personal, it made her seem increasingly out of touch with France's financial troubles and social unrest.

Marie's upbringing and education had focused on courtly life rather than practical governance, leaving her unprepared for the economic crises her country faced. Her continued lavish spending and disconnect from the realities of her subjects contributed to her image as a symbol of excess and made her a target during the Revolution. Though she never likely said "Let them eat cake," the phrase captured the public's perception of her detachment.

Marie Antoinette's way of thinking is a classic example of the "Idols of the Cave." Her upbringing and fixation in luxury shaped her worldview, which limited her ability to understand and empathize with France's financial struggles and social unrest.

According to Bacon, The Idol of the Cave can make people superficial and lazy in their pursuit of truth, unwilling to question other ideas. It also forces people to sacrifice their

---

[22] *Research guides: France: Women in the Revolution: Marie Antoinette*. (n.d.). https://guides.loc.gov/women-in-the-french-revolution/marie-antoinette

personal skills and beliefs to conform to an institution's values and dogma. In Marie Antoinette's case, this is seen in her focus on royal expectations rather than practical approaches to governance.

Idols of The Marketplace.

In George Orwell's *1984*, Oceania is ruled by the Party that uses propaganda and "doublespeak" to control and manipulate the public. This is exemplified through slogans like "War is Peace," "Freedom is Slavery," and "Ignorance is Strength." These contradictory statements are designed to confuse and suppress critical thinking by presenting conflicting ideas as simultaneously true.

The Party also develops Newspeak, a controlled language designed to shut down rebellious thoughts. By simplifying vocabulary—like using "plus good" instead of "very good"—Newspeak limits the ways people can express dissent or even think for themselves.

The Party's manipulation of language in 1984 is a prime example of how the Idols of the Marketplace function. This type relates to propaganda by focusing on the abuse of language to diminish people's critical thinking.

Bacon also argues that misuse of language can make science and philosophy contradictory and ultimately meaningless.

Idols of The Theater.

During the Middle Ages, Claudius Ptolemy's geocentric model[23] was widely accepted, placing Earth at the center of the universe with celestial bodies orbiting it in complex epicycles.

Despite emerging evidence from astronomers like Copernicus and Galileo challenging this model, the Ptolemaic system persisted within academic and religious institutions. This was due in part to a resistance to question established ideas that aligned with contemporary theological and philosophical views.

This reluctance is exemplified by the fourth idol, the Idol of the Theater. This type represents the unquestioning acceptance of ancient texts and the failure to critically assess or update them.

This is a distinctly Renaissance idea; the academic culture of the Middle Ages held the teachings of philosophers like Aristotle dear and copied them unquestioningly. Renaissance thinkers began to question old academic dogma in Bacon's time and made prominent advances in science, literature, art, and philosophy. Bacon was an ardent advocate for progressive ideas like these,

---

23 Dobrijevic, D. (2021, December 17). *Geocentric model: The Earth-centered view of the universe.* Space.com. https://www.space.com/geocentric-model

which he practiced in developing his new empirical scientific methods.

Identify Bacon's Idols of the Mind.

Identify Francis Bacon's "Idols of the Mind"—Tribe, Cave, Marketplace, and Theater—by recognizing how they influence the thinking and decision-making of each person in each scenario.

Scenario 1:
Sarah lives in a small rural town where most people believe that genetically modified crops are dangerous. Without researching, she assumes that GMOs must be harmful simply because the majority in her community think so.
Which Idol?

____

Explanation:

____

Scenario 2:
During a marketing meeting, Anna argues that the term "viral" should only refer to content that spreads rapidly on social media, even though others suggest that the term could also apply to organic growth over time. She dismisses these interpretations because "everyone else" uses it to mean rapid spread.
Which Idol?

____

Explanation:

____

Scenario 3:

James, a university student, passionately adheres to a particular economic theory that his professor promotes. He dismisses alternative economic models presented by other professors as irrelevant, without exploring them, because he trusts his professor's expertise unquestioningly.

Which Idol?

____

Explanation:

____

Scenario 4:

Tom, an experienced accountant, insists on using manual bookkeeping methods because his mentor always did it that way. Despite colleagues showing him more efficient software, he refuses to switch, convinced that the traditional way is superior.

Which Idol?

____

Explanation:

____

How to Destroy the Idols.[24]

To overcome each idol, Bacon proposes a two-pronged approach:

1. We must recognize these idols for what they are—biases that distort our understanding. Acknowledging our inherent prejudices is crucial, even though complete freedom from them is unattainable.

   For instance, if you find yourself assuming that people will like your ideas or decisions simply because they align with popular trends or opinions, you might be influenced by the Idol of the Tribe. To counter this, make a conscious effort to evaluate your ideas independently of social pressures.

2. We should rely on "true induction" and "common logic" to form our ideas. While eliminating all cognitive biases is unlikely, relying on logic and rationality offers the best route to clarity.

   For example, if you're making a significant life decision, like choosing a career path, instead of relying solely on gut feelings or external opinions, use logical reasoning and gather concrete evidence. Create a list of pros and cons, seek out unbiased advice, and consider the long-term impacts of your choice.

---

[24] Thomson, J. (2022, April 19). Francis Bacon and the four barriers to truth. Big Think. https://bigthink.com/thinking/cognitive-bias-francis-bacon-idols/

Bacon's Inductive Reasoning.

Bacon's inductive method[25] came from the idea that natural substances can be understood as aggregates of simpler, fundamental components known as "simple natures." This approach assumes that by analyzing these basic elements, we can get a clearer understanding of more complex substances.

In simple terms, Bacon's method transforms observations into empirical inquiries through systematic observation and experimentation. By looking at how these simple natures interact in various substances, we can develop general principles or theories. This process involves spotting patterns and consistencies, which helps us build broader theories.

To effectively practice induction in everyday thinking, you must do the following steps:

1. Start with a broad hypothesis or educated guess about something you're curious about or trying to understand.

2. Gather reliable resources. Ensure your observations or data collection methods are accurate and free from bias to avoid skewed results.

[25] Belkind, Ori. (2021). Bacon's Inductive Method and Material Form. 58. 57-68.

3. Use your observations to reason toward a broader conclusion but stay within the limits of your collected data.

4. Continue gathering more information, including differing opinions, similar findings, and other people's observations. This helps strengthen and refine your initial hypothesis.

5. With additional data, revisit your hypothesis. Adjust your conclusions based on new evidence, conflicting theories, and any new insights you've gained.

6. Keep repeating these steps—collecting data, analyzing it, and refining your conclusions. Over time, you'll develop a well-supported conclusion based on solid, objective evidence.

Bacon believed this was the only way people could truly learn about the world around them. Furthermore, its turn away from the deduction methods used by the ancients (such as Aristotle) meant people could start over and question long-held beliefs in the name of intellectual progress. This is, of course, a fundamentally Renaissance idea.[26]

Apply Bacon's Inductive Reasoning.

---

[26] Matthews, Professor Steven (2013). Theology and Science in the Thought of Francis Bacon. Ashgate Publishing, Ltd. ISBN 9781409480143.

Learn to use Bacon's method of inductive reasoning to form a conclusion based on observations.

Step 1: Pick a broad hypothesis or an educated guess about how something works.

Example: “Exercise improves mood.”

Your hypothesis:

____

Step 2: Gather information through observations or research. Make sure your data is relevant and unbiased. For example, find studies or make observations about how exercise affects mood.

Observations:____

____

____

____

Step 3: Look for patterns in your data that support your hypothesis. Don't draw conclusions beyond what your data shows. For example, determine if most studies or observations show a link between exercise and improved mood.

Data analysis:

____

____

____

____

____

____

____

Step 4: Find more data to strengthen your conclusion. This includes looking for evidence that supports or challenges your hypothesis. For instance, explore if there are cases where exercise doesn't improve mood or only helps in certain situations.

Additional data analysis:

____

____

____

____

Step 5: Based on all the evidence, write a conclusion that is fully supported by your data. For instance, summarize your findings, sticking only to what your data shows about the link between exercise and mood.

Your conclusion:

____

____

____

____

Chapter 4: René Descartes

> "If when I don't perceive the truth vividly and clearly enough I simply suspend judgment, it's clear that I am behaving correctly and avoiding error. It is a misuse of my free will to have an opinion in such cases: if I choose the wrong side I shall be in error; and even if I choose the right side, I shall be at fault because I'll have come to the truth by sheer chance and not through a perception of my intellect." – Rene Descartes

Background.

"Je pense, donc je suis" — "I think, therefore I am" This is the first quote that comes to mind for many people when they think about René Descartes. Indeed, Descartes was one of the most important critical thinkers of the European Renaissance, and his book *Rules for the Direction of the Mind* is widely considered a canonical text in the field.

Descartes believed in a disciplined approach to critical thinking, aimed at producing clear and precise thoughts. His method was based on what we call "systematic doubt," which means every step of thinking needs to be put under thorough examination. You can think of it as a more elaborate Socratic method. This approach focused on three key actions: question, doubt, test.[27]

In his *Rules for the Direction of the Mind,* Descartes divides these principles into three main parts. The first 12 rules lay out the groundwork for understanding science, focusing on how we process information through intuition, deduction, and careful review. He also talks about "simple propositions," those basic truths that come to us naturally and are clearly understood, like knowing that a triangle is made up of just three lines.[28]

Descartes was born in 1596, when the Renaissance was well underway in Europe, and died in 1650. He delvcd into mathematics, philosophy, and the sciences, establishing himself as an intellectual radical early in his career. His scientific work was part of the Scientific Revolution, which had started about fifty years before his birth with Copernicus and stretched into the 18th century Enlightenment.

Philosophically, Descartes helped develop rationalism—a school of thought championed by Spinoza and contrasting with Francis Bacon's empiricism. Rationalism, unlike empiricism, relied on intellectual deductions and disdained sensory data. This was similar to precepts found in Aristotelian philosophy. Though

---

[27] Custom Writing Tips. (2018) The Importance of Critical Thinking. Custom Writing Tips. https://customwritingtips.com/component/k2/item/9848-the-importance-of-critical-thinking.html?tmpl=component&print=1

[28] Dika, Tarek R., "Descartes' Method", The Stanford Encyclopedia of Philosophy (Summer 2024 Edition), Edward N. Zalta & Uri Nodelman (eds.), https://plato.stanford.edu/archives/sum2024/entries/descartes-method/

rationalism later got tied to atheism and opposition to religious institutions, Descartes himself wasn't aiming for that end.

Descartes often turned his attention to the nature of reality, which ties back to his famous quote "I think, therefore I am." He conducted thought experiments and often assumed that all of reality was just a dream, given that dreams allow us to experience physical sensations. To navigate this, he used critical reasoning, doubting everything until he reached a fundamental truth.

Understanding perspective was often the key; for instance, he considered how a table can appear different colors in different light and used this to create a way to judge false appearances from the real nature of things. Just as you can figure out through reasoning that your observations are wrong and the table is actually one color, you can figure out the true nature of things by using your mind. This observation flew directly in the face of both empiricists and skeptics who believed real knowledge was beyond reach.

Descartes's practice of doubt extended to thought experiments like *The Matrix*, where reality could be produced by demon inducing visions in the brain. Through these explorations, he reached a conclusion: although he could never be certain about the nature of reality, he could be certain he himself was doing all this thinking. He thought, therefore, he existed. Building on this foundation, Descartes determined that other knowledge beyond doubt could be produced and began to promote the mind's creativity as a generative force for knowledge. This led to the development of the Philosophy of Caution, otherwise known as philosophy of absolute certainty.

Descartes and Critical Thinking.[29]

Descartes laid out four principles in his book *Discourse on Method* for proper critical thinking. But before applying these principles, it's crucial to have a clear understanding of the idea you're reasoning about. Begin by carefully analyzing the subject to get to the heart of it. Only after this step can you start the process of critical thinking.

First, you must never jump to conclusions. This means you can't say something is true without having absolute certainty that it is true. You must question all ideas, regardless of whether they're wildly outside the norm or well-established. Only after you've thoroughly examined an idea and reached absolute certainty should you accept it as true and move forward.

The second principle is dividing up any problems you encounter within an idea into the smallest pieces possible. This way, you can handle each part more effectively, sort through the issues faster, and get on to the next task.

---

[29] Boammaaruri. (2017) René Descartes on critical thinking and avoiding error in judgments. https://boammaaruri.blog/2017/05/15/rene-descartes-on-critical-thinking-and-avoiding-error-in-judgments/

The third principle is to begin with the simplest steps in your critical thinking and move on to the more complicated ideas later. This approach will help you keep your thoughts in order and build a secure foundation of truth before tackling more uncertain pieces of knowledge.

Lastly, the fourth principle is to make your final idea as thorough as possible. This means that you should include the details from your thought process to make sure nothing's been overlooked. Doing so gives you the most solid evidence to back up the conclusions you've drawn from your critical thinking process.

The Escape Room Challenge Exercise.

You find yourself in an old, dimly lit study room with creaky wooden floors and shelves full of dusty books. A large oak desk sits in the center of the room, covered in scattered papers and strange objects. In one corner, there's a locked box with a combination lock, and on the wall, a framed note with cryptic numbers. A grandfather clock ticks softly in the background, and the faint smell of old leather and parchment fills the air.

Use Descartes' principles to tackle each puzzle.

Puzzle 1: Avoid Jumping to Conclusions.

You find a locked box with a combination lock. There is a note on the wall with the numbers 7, 12, and 5. It looks like the combination might be 7-12-5, but before you decide, you need to explore the room further.

Before deciding the combination might be 7-12-5. Examine the room for additional hints or clues. Check the desk, the bookshelf, and even under the rug.

What additional clues or evidence did you find?

- ______________________________
- ______________________________

Possible alternative combinations based on your findings:

- ______________________________
- ______________________________

Puzzle 2: Break Down thc Problem.

You try the combination, but the lock won't budge. You notice that the lock has three dials, each with numbers from 0 to 9. Could it be that the lock has a different number of dials than you initially thought?

Break down the problem by listing possible issues with the lock. Is it a three-digit lock or something else? Are there any hidden compartments or additional clues?

List out the different factors and clues related to the lock:

- ______________________________
- ______________________________

What adjustments did you make to resolve the issue?

- ____________________________________
- ____________________________________

Puzzle 3: Start with Simple Steps.

On the desk, you find a series of letters: "QWERTY." There's also an old typewriter with some keys missing. Could the letters be a clue?

Start by testing straightforward combinations using the letters you have. Try simple substitutions or direct combinations before tackling more complex arrangements.

What simple combinations did you test?

- ____________________________________
- ____________________________________

Did any straightforward solutions work? If so, what was the solution?

- ____________________________________
- ____________________________________

Puzzle 4: Make Your Conclusion Complete.

After solving several puzzles, you find a final riddle written on a dusty old scroll: "The sum of all numbers found equals the key."

Gather all the numbers and clues you've collected throughout the room. Calculate the total sum to ensure your final answer for the escape room is accurate.

Numbers and clues collected:

- ______________________________________
- ______________________________________

Sum of all numbers:

- ______________________________________

Final answer for the escape room:

- ______________________________________

After you've "escaped" the room, take a moment to reflect on the process. How did using Descartes' principles help you in solving the puzzles? Did any principle make the process easier or clearer? How can you apply these principles to everyday problem-solving?

- ____
- ____

In tackling the mystery room, you put Descartes' four principles of critical thinking to work: questioning everything, breaking problems down, starting with simple solutions, and being thorough. This hands-on exercise showed how careful, methodical thinking clears up complex issues and helps solve problems effectively.

Descartes also pointed out that our will, driven by personal motives and desires, often skews our critical thinking. Much like how jumping to conclusions or misleading clues in the escape room could throw you off, our will can muddy judgment with biases and incomplete information.

Descartes noted that our will forms opinions and beliefs about things before we've properly reasoned out the truth. Unlike the intellect, which relies on reason, the will is influenced by desires and passions. Thus, to uncover the truth, we must rely on the intellect and reason to determine the truth instead of judgments made by the will.

Descartes also understood that being social creatures affects our thinking. Public opinion and social pressures can lead us to accept beliefs without proper scrutiny, driven by our evolutionary desire to fit in. Although Descartes wasn't aware of evolution, he recognized that our social nature often sways our beliefs, making us follow popular or inherited views without critical examination.

For example, people often vote for a popular party or one their parents support without thoroughly evaluating the party's platform. This reflects how social influences can sway our will, leading us to accept ideas without critical reasoning. Again, the will has supplanted the intellect in a process that would be better governed by critical thinking. Pre-existing biases and the desire to fit in can ultimately lead to errors in thinking, and Descartes believed the solution was iconoclastic critical thinking like his own process.

The Cartesian Method.

Descartes made his mark early on by leaving his law studies in 1616 to focus solely on philosophy, a bold move that showcased his independent spirit. He felt the leadership of his university wanted to mold him in their image to serve their own interests instead of allowing him to form his own body of knowledge. So, he decided to reexamine everything he'd learned, starting from scratch to seek the truth. This approach gave rise to what we now call the Cartesian Method, detailed in his *Meditations*.

In his First Meditation, Descartes set out to doubt everything he knew to find what was absolutely certain. He realized that the purpose of doubting was to find knowledge that was irrefutably true. By questioning everything, he aimed to distinguish lasting truths from uncertainties. This purposive doubt, rather than existential questioning, would eventually lead to lasting advances in science, philosophy, and Descartes's other pursuits.

The practice of purposive doubt was not to throw out all previous knowledge, but to examine it all to determine what was true and what needed revision. Indeed, Descartes was willing to entertain the idea that some knowledge was actually true.

Descartes's quest for certainty is still relevant today. Technology may speed up information sharing, but it's essential to critically examine these opinions to find objective truth. Descartes would have advocated for rigorous investigation rather than accepting Internet commentary at face value. He valued certainty so highly because he knew it was critical. Once you're completely certain of what you know after critical investigation, you will be better at making decisions about news you share, services you perform, charitable causes you donate to, and your civic activities.

Certainty makes knowledge more satisfying. Think about watching a movie in which you recognize an actor. If you were to say to your companion, "I think that is so-and-so, but I'm not one hundred percent sure," it would probably bother both you and the person you're watching with. You might even look it up online during the movie. Certainty removes that frustration and eliminates doubts. Descartes was aware that certainty and knowledge are intrinsically related. Without certainty, all knowledge remains suspect, making it crucial to establish.

Test Your Beliefs with Cartesian Doubt.

Dive into Descartes' method and see if your beliefs hold up.

- **Choose a Belief:** Pick a common opinion or belief you hold—whether it's about a trend, a political stance, or something everyone seems to accept.

  ____

  ____

  ____

- **Get to Questioning:**

  What's the core of this belief?

  ____

  What assumptions are at its heart?

  ____

  ____

  ____

  ____

  ____

- **Trace Its Roots.**

  Where did you pick this belief up? Was it through personal experience, something you were taught, or just what everyone else thinks?

- **Spot the Influences.**

Are there any biases or outside pressures that might have influenced you?

- **Break It Down.**

Split the belief into smaller parts. Can you challenge or disprove any of these parts?

- **Rebuild Your Understanding.**

Based on what you've found, reassess your belief. Is it still solid, or does it need some adjustment?

- **Reflect and Share.**
    - Note down how this process affected your belief and what new insights you've gained
    - Share your findings with friends or family and see how they respond!

Doubt and the Cartesian Method.

Descartes made a groundbreaking realization: our senses can deceive us. Just consider optical illusions or hallucinations—what we perceive isn't always reality. What people say, what we see, and what we feel can all be unreliable. Thus, we must rely on reason to uncover the true nature of reality. This rational approach contrasts with Baconian empiricism, which we discussed earlier, but complements it by adding a layer of reason to our observations.

Descartes himself noted, *"Sometimes towers which have looked round from a distance appeared square from a close up; and enormous statues standing on their pediments did not seem large when observed from the ground. In these and countless other such cases, I find that judgments of the external senses were mistaken." (Meditation IV)*

In his later Meditations, Descartes grew increasingly skeptical of his own reality. In Meditation XI, he extended his doubt to even his own memory, sense-perceptions, actions, and body. These elements of his perceived reality could be nothing more than an elaborate illusion, possibly orchestrated by a higher power. While he achieved the existential certainty of "I think, therefore I am," many aspects of reality remained uncertain.

Ultimately, Descartes's Cartesian Method emphasizes the importance of an open and questioning mind. Since we've already covered the specifics of the Cartesian Method in earlier sections, let's reflect on its practical aspects. Descartes laid out four key steps in his *Discourse on Method*:

1. Don't take something as 'true' unless it is clear and recognizable as such.
2. Divide and conquer with your reasoning — break down problems into their smallest parts to make them manageable.
3. Start at the simplest form of knowledge and build up to more complex ideas.
4. Stay updated and revisit your method to ensure your knowledge remains certain and complete.

Descartes asserted that seeking truth through critical thinking requires questioning everything, including basic beliefs learned early in life. By re-examining and breaking down these beliefs into smaller parts, we can assess their validity and rebuild our knowledge on a solid foundation.

His First Meditation sets the stage for this process of critical scrutiny.

Cartesian doubt has two key aspects for thinkers:

1. It is an analytic-heuristic model of critical thinking based on conceptual thinking.
2. It begins with simple reasoning and builds up to more complex thought processes.

The Cartesian Method is such an important model of critical thinking because it is one of the fundamental pillars of the Philosophy of Caution, which is central to the discipline of critical thinking. By questioning everything, it provides a framework for rigorous inquiry, accessible to both everyday individuals and philosophers alike.

Chapter 5: Immanuel Kant

Background.

Immanuel Kant (1724-1804) was a German philosopher known for his contribution to moral philosophy, ethics, and of course, critical thinking. He believed that our morality comes from our ability to reason, meaning we can use reason to make morally correct choices in our daily lives.

In his book *Critique of Pure Reason*, published in 1781, Kant theorized a way to fix the issues in metaphysics and philosophy and to establish a link between reason and humanity, all while avoiding skepticism which was popular among his contemporaries. He saw his philosophy as a solution to the divide between rationalists, like Descartes, and the empiricists like Bacon, as we discussed in the last chapter.

Kant proposed that experiences are shaped by the necessary aspects of the human mind to the degree that all human experience shares the same basic structural features. These features included concepts of space, time, cause, and effect. Therefore, he reasoned that our experiences are always mediated by our senses, limiting our access to the "noumenal world," or the innate nature of the things.

Kant also believed that the main purpose of critical thinking was not to justify knowledge but to provide criticism. A critical thinker shouldn't seek knowledge itself, but *rather judge the possibilities and limitations of knowledge*. Philosophers shouldn't theorize about the nature of reality; they should critically investigate every existing theory and the discipline itself. If these theories fail to withstand criticism, then their validity should be questioned.

This practice is often called "critical philosophy." Kant wanted to evaluate the human experience rather than Descartes's abstract notion of "reality." He believed that carefully analyzing human reason was required before attempting to understand anything else.

Kant recommended starting by examining how reason works and identifying its weaknesses. Next, use this understanding to evaluate sensory experiences and determine if reason applies to other areas. This is a clear fusion of rationalism and empiricism, in that it marries the two by mediating with reason.[30]

Kant and Critical Thinking.[31]

In the essay "What is Enlightenment?" Kant articulates his views on critical thinking quite clearly. For him, "enlightenment" happens when humans free themselves from "immaturity," which he defined as the inability to use

---

[30] Frederick C. Beiser, (2002) German Idealism: The Struggle Against Subjectivism, 1781-1801, Harvard University Press.

[31] Kantian School. (2012) Immanuel Kant and Critical Thinking. http://kantianschool.blogspot.com/2012/02/immanuel-kant-and-critical-thinking.html

your reason without someone else's guidance. To think critically, you must be willing and able to think for yourself.

However, Kant knew that cultivating this mentality is not easy. In fact, he believed people were mentally lazy, unwilling to think for themselves. It is, after all, much easier to let someone do the lion's share of thinking for you. Taking the things you read or that other people tell you for granted is part of this. Instead of questioning the information they absorb, people prefer being told what to think.

But Kant's solution to this problem was not to cease seeking new information entirely. He believed people should investigate every piece of knowledge they absorb thoroughly, examining alternatives to find what the truth is. This comes back to the basic principles of critical thinking established by Socrates, but Kant expanded on them by considering people's basic natures.

Of course, this doesn't mean questioning should become too unconventional or dangerous in certain contexts. For example, an emergency medical technician can't use anything poisonous as a medicine for the sake of "trying it out". Instead, technicians must follow the precepts of being an EMT and stick to training and the scope of knowledge in the field. Otherwise, people could be put in harm's way. Similarly, if you are running a track relay race, you still need to hand off the baton correctly, otherwise you'll be disqualified for cheating. Kant called these contexts "private use of one's reason."

However, public use of reason needs to be exercised freely, without restraint. This sort of use is primarily academic, as found in scholarly debate. Free public use of reason is necessary for scholars because they need to be able to question the existing authorities and precepts in their disciplines.

Without this freedom, the pursuit of new knowledge would be stifled. When scholars aren't free to question existing scholarship, it can lead to dangerous censorship and ostracism within the community, ultimately harming our collective knowledge. This was a big issue in Kant's time, and it wasn't until the twentieth century that scholars could freely express their own opinions without risking their careers.

Despite this, scholars-in-training still face barriers to exercising the full public use of their reason. If students fear displeasing their professors, they might hold back from expressing a new idea contradicting that professor's work. Ideally, the scholarly realm should regularly exercise free expression within reason, as this is where the best critical thinking takes place.

Private use of reason is important in contexts where consensus is necessary but questioning what can be questioned is still a good general policy. For example, an EMT must scrutinize a colleague's technique if they think it's wrong. In this sense, critical thinking can be applied in any context and position, making it a necessary skill for people from all walks of life.

Kantian Philosophy.[32]

Kant's key philosophical quest in life was to understand the limits of reason and human knowledge. Defining these limits would help future scholars have an idea of what can be investigated with reason.

Kant's ideas about reason were revolutionary, as they acknowledged how our minds influence our observations. The mind doesn't receive unfiltered information; instead, it filters information through our own experiences so we can interpret and mentally process them. This acknowledgment of personal bias allows us to distinguish between our perceptions, which we know, and reality, or *noumena*, which we can never wholly know due to these biases.

Kant also defined judgments from prior experience, or *a priori*, and judgments based on sensory perception, or *a posteriori*. These categories of judgment can be used to critically reason through difficult metaphysical problems like free will, the existence/independence of the soul, death, and life after death, and even the existence and nature of God. Kant's most famous idea, however, was that of the *categorical imperative*.

---

[32] Brook, Andrew, "Kant's View of the Mind and Consciousness of Self", *The Stanford Encyclopedia of Philosophy* (Winter 2018 Edition), Edward N. Zalta. https://plato.stanford.edu/archives/win2018/entries/kant-mind/

Categorical Imperative.

The categorical imperative is the ethical theory suggesting that the right way to act is in a manner that one would be comfortable with everyone else doing as well.

For example, if you consider lying to friends about why you can't attend their party, the categorical imperative asks if you'd be okay with everyone lying in the same situation. Since universal lying would lead to damaged trust, you should choose to be honest.

While the categorical imperative and the golden rule may seem similar, they differ fundamentally. The golden rule urges you to treat others as you'd like to be treated, focusing on personal reciprocity. The categorical imperative, on the other hand, requires you to act according to principles you'd want everyone to follow universally.

These distinctions lead to different outcomes. For example, the categorical imperative might compel you to never skip a line, as you believe everyone should follow that rule. In contrast, the golden rule might lead you to let someone go ahead if you'd appreciate the same courtesy in their place.

Using the Categorical Imperative.[33]

In critical thinking, the categorical imperative is used to evaluate the ethical soundness of decisions and arguments. Here are steps to do it properly:

1. **Consider, "How would you feel if everyone acted this way?"**

If you're thinking about exaggerating your qualifications on a job application, ask yourself how you'd feel if everyone did the same. This self-distancing approach helps you assess the integrity of your action.

2. **Imagine what it would look like if everyone behaved the same way you are considering.**

Let's say you're considering taking credit for someone else's work, visualize a world where everyone claims others' achievements. This helps you understand the broader impact of your actions.

3. **Evaluate the potential short-term and long-term effects if everyone followed the same principle.**

Thinking of avoiding your responsibilities at work? Consider the immediate effects on your team and the long-term impact on workplace trust and productivity. This makes sure your actions align with universal ethical standards.

---

[33] Shatz, I. (n.d.). *Kant's categorical imperative: Act the way you want others to act.* https://effectiviology.com/categorical-imperative/#How_to_use_the_categorical_imperative

The Categorical Imperative Exercise.

Use the following guide questions to practice applying the categorical imperative and evaluate the validity of decisions or actions.

1. **What specific decision or action are you contemplating right now?**

____

____

____

____

____

2. **How would you feel if everyone acted this way?**

____

____

____

____

____

3. **What would it look like if everyone behaved the same way you are considering?**

____

____

____

____

____

4. **What are the short-term and long-term effects if everyone followed the same principle?**

____

____

____

____

____

Phenomena and Noumena.

Kant's theory, a critically reasoned approach, contrasts with Scottish empiricist David Hume's view, which asserts that knowledge comes solely from sense perception. Hume argued that space, time, and causality are mental constructs rather than objective realities.

Recognizing that the mind limits understanding, Kant expanded on Hume's work to explore these limits and their implications. He called the things we experience and derive our knowledge from *phenomena*, as opposed to *noumena*.

To interpret phenomena, our minds need to impose certain structures on them. Kant concluded that our minds therefore have such structural-interpretive abilities, which make reality perceptible to us.

The most important of these structures are time and space. Space helps determine the relationships between objects, while time organizes events as a sequence. These structures help us make sense of what we perceive on the most fundamental level, allowing us to focus on complex ideas. Similarly, our perceptions of cause and effect helps us order events to understand why things happen.

Substance, or existence, is another concept our minds have created for us to function within our reality. When we perceive something, we consider perception as evidence of the object's existence. This allows us to conceive of the reality we perceive as something existentially real, which, in turn, helps us to interact better with it.

These types of mental ordering help us understand our perceptions, but they're no help in determining the true nature of reality.

To Kant, since we can never fully grasp the true nature of reality, we cannot truly understand God, our world, or our souls, all of which fall under the category of *noumena*. Although we've created these ideas based on things we've perceived, this is not proof that they exist.

This contrasts with Descartes's view, which asserts that things, including God, exist because they exist as ideas in our minds. Despite our lack of knowledge of these things, we do know the experiences we have had and can learn the experiences of others, which still creates a wide body of knowledge.

Analytic and Synthetic Judgments.

According to Kant, every statement of knowledge comes with a judgment about that piece of knowledge. These judgments come in several forms, some of which have already been brought up.

A key distinction is the difference between analytic and synthetic judgments. Analytic judgments are what we think of as obvious statements, for example, “dogs are animals.” This isn't revelatory information, but it tells you what was implied by the subject of the statement.

Analytic judgments are those that, if negated, would be a contradiction. Think about it: you could never say “dogs are not animals” without getting strange looks. This is your key to telling whether a judgment is analytic.

Synthetic judgments, on the other hand, tell you additional information about the subject of the logical sentence. For example, you could say “that dress is green” is a synthetic judgment. The color of the dress, green, is a new piece of information added to the subject, the dress. The key in synthetic judgments is that they can be negated and still logically consistent.

If you say, “that dress is not green,” you're not stating something logically contradictory. Therefore, the “new piece” in any synthetic judgment can be true or not true and will be logically sound regardless.

Identify Synthetic and Analytic Judgments.

Read each statement and determine if it is synthetic or analytic. After identifying the type, explain why you made that choice.

Ex. "All triangles have three sides."

It is an analytic judgment because the predicate "three sides" is included in the definition of "triangle" and does not require empirical observation.

a. "All squares have four sides."

____

____

____

____

b. "The book is on the table."

____

____

____

____

c. "A triangle has three sides."

____

____

____

____

d. "Some flowers are red."

____

____

e. "All bachelors are unmarried men."

A Priori and A Posteriori.[34]

When combining the previous types of judgments with *a priori* and *a posteriori* judgments, you get a good idea of how our mind organizes our experiences. But first, let's define them:

A priori judgments or claims are based solely on reason and logic, independent of any sensory experience. Because they are derived from pure thought, they apply universally and with strict consistency. For example, mathematical truths like "1 + 2 = 3" are known a priori because they are understood through reasoning alone.

In contrast, a posteriori judgments rely on sensory experience and empirical evidence. As a result, they are limited and can vary based on specific observations. For

[34] *Epistemology: A Priori vs. A posteriori; Analytic vs. Synthetic, Necessary vs. Contingent - Lucid Philosophy.* (2017b, September 14). Lucid Philosophy. https://lucidphilosophy.com/1019-2/

instance, "The coffee is hot" is a posteriori because it is based on direct sensory experience and may differ depending on individual observations.

Therefore, while a priori judgments provide universal and certain knowledge, a posteriori judgments offer insights that are contingent on experience and subject to variation.

Identify A priori and A posteriori.

Read each statement and determine whether it is a priori (based on reason alone and universally true) or a posteriori (based on sensory experience and empirical evidence). After identifying the type, provide an explanation.

Example: All triangles have three sides.

It's an a priori because this is a definitional truth about geometric shapes.

1. The sun is currently shining in New York City.

____

____

____

____

2. If all humans are mortal and Socrates is a human, then Socrates is mortal.

____

____

____

____

3. People often enjoy eating ice cream on hot days.

____

____

____

____

4. All even numbers are divisible by 2.

____

____

____

____

5. Cats often purr when they are content.

____

____

____

____

Synthetic A Priori Judgment.

According to Kant, our mind organizes our experiences by making synthetic *a priori* judgments. We process our information using what we already know independent of our sensory experiences, combined with adding new information on to what we already know.

In other words, we synthesize our existing knowledge base with our new sensory observations. We then put this process into a “’category’, like cause and effect, to make it more digestible. The very concept of cause and effect is a synthetic *a priori* judgment because we assume the world has meaning and observe that certain things follow others. By imposing this observation on our existing knowledge of ‘purpose’, we conclude that there are causes and effects in the world.

By explicating this process of acquiring knowledge and clearly defining the boundaries of human knowledge, Kant aimed to end the debate around metaphysical questions like whether God exists. His goal was to show the philosophical community that such questions were not within the bounds of human knowledge, and the debate would not be worth the time.

However, Kant didn’t necessarily believe religion was wrong. He still thought some beliefs were worthwhile even if they were not one hundred percent certain. Belief in a higher power like God, or in heaven, helps people cope with their everyday struggles, and Kant wrote in the *Critique of Practical Reason* that this was a worthy reason to hold an uncertain belief. Practical beliefs can be as useful as critically reasoned truths, and Kant also realized people could have emotional truths as well as rational ones.

Kant's moral philosophy was even more well-known. He believed morality derives from having a “good will” instead of every individual action you make, and that we each have a duty to perform actions from this “good will.” Wanting to do good is not enough to be a good person; you actually have to feel an obligation to always be good, instead of just performing good actions on a whim.

Following this duty, the “categorical imperative,” is what really determines whether someone is a good person, not thinking nice thoughts or donating to charity once a year. You have the duty to perform an action if you know it is right, and you shouldn't have any other motivation if you want to be truly good.

The way we know what is right through our *a priori* judgments. We don't have to observe good actions to know what the right thing to do is.

According to Kant, what is right is universally so and therefore right for all people at all times. This goes back to our previously discussed definition of the categorical imperative. This standard is an easy way to determine the morality of actions; if you wouldn't want someone to steal from you, for example, you should never steal. The categorical imperative is a highly practical, if not the exclusive, system for moral determination.

Chapter 6: John Stuart Mill

"The only way in which a human being can make some approach to knowing the whole of a subject, is by hearing what can be said about it by persons of every variety of opinion, and studying all modes in which it can be looked at by every character of mind."

- John Stuart Mill, *On Liberty*, 1859

Background.

Born in Great Britain in 1806 and passing away in 1873, John Stuart Mill was one of the great philosophers of his era. In addition to his philosophical work, he served as a civil servant and political economist. Recognized as a pioneer of liberalism, Mill championed individual freedom over state and societal control. An early suffragist and politician in Parliament, many of his ideas were far ahead of his time.

Educated by his father, James Mill, and the renowned philosopher Jeremy Bentham, John Stuart Mill was socially isolated from other children during his upbringing, dedicating most of his energy to learning. His father, a committed utilitarian, shaped him into the next great

Utilitarian thinker, taking up Bentham's legacy and further developing the school of thought.

Education.

As a result of his childhood, John Stuart Mill was intensely interested in education. He wrote extensively about the methods his father used, which, though often harsh by today's standards, offer intriguing insights into training a mind to become a great critical thinker.

This method focused on disciplining and developing the mind. With his son being his only student, James Mill put all his energy into training young John Stuart to think critically using specific and difficult techniques.

James knew that acquiring knowledge was a long process, composed of a good repository of important knowledge. He then trained John Stuart to examine these ideas by comparing them to others, applying them, and exploring new solutions. His goal for his son was for him to take real ownership of his thoughts and his thought process, ultimately gaining complete understanding of things.[35]

The strongest aspects of this teaching strategy achieved what effective teaching should: it engaged the young John Stuart Mill in his learning, enabling him to think independently as he studied and wrote about his areas of interest.

---

[35] Ralph Raico (2018). Mises Institute, ed. "John Stuart Mill and the New Liberalism".

The more specific methodology, drawn from his writings, is outlined below:

- Mill self-directed his own reading, then talked with his father while taking walks in nature about what he had read.
- He always prepared notes from his readings then used them to discuss with his father on their walks. This combination of self-direction, deep discussion, and fresh air can do wonders for critical thinking.
- During these talks, Mill received explanations from his father about important ideas–ranging from politics to moral philosophy. After this, Mill repeated them back to his father in his own words. This was to ensure that he understood these ideas for himself.
- Additionally, Mill read books that were recommended by his father to broaden his knowledge outside of his known interests. He read the works of Plato, Demosthenes, David Ricardo, and Adam Smith.
- To further sharpen his critical thinking, Mill taught what learned to his younger siblings, who then reported the lesson back to their father.

Learn Like John Stuart Mill.

Now, put yourself in the shoes of John Stuart Mill and learn just like he did. Complete the following exercises to enhance critical thinking, deepen comprehension, and expand your knowledge.

1. Choose Your Topic:

Select a topic of personal interest. Read a book or article on the subject and take detailed notes as you read. Focus on key points, questions that arise, and any new ideas you encounter.

Book/Topic Chosen:

____

Notes:

____

____

____

____

Questions/Reflections:

____

____

____

____

2. Broaden Your Horizon.

Have someone (a mentor, friend, or family member) assign you a book or article on a subject you wouldn’t typically choose. Engage with this material fully by taking the same kind of notes as you did for your self-directed reading.

Notes:

____

____

____

____

Questions/Reflections:

____

____

____

____

3. Walk-and-Talk Session.

Arrange a walk with a partner (mentor, friend, or family member). Bring your notes from both readings.

During the walk, explain what you've learned from both readings in your own words. Dive into both the subject you chose and the one assigned to you. Encourage your partner to ask you clarifying questions or challenge you on certain points.

Summary of Key Points from Discussion:

____

____

____

____

Questions/Challenges from Partner:

____

____

____

____

Your Responses:

____

____

____

____

____

4. Reflect and Rephrase.

After the discussion, reflect on the feedback you received and rephrase key concepts or points. This will help ensure you deeply understand the material.

Rephrased Key Concepts:

____

____

____

____

5. Memory Reinforcement.

At the end of your walk, take a few minutes to summarize the key ideas you discussed without referring to your notes. Repeating information in your own words will help solidify your understanding and aid long-term memory.

Summary of Key Ideas in Your Own Words:

____

____

____

____

6. Teaching Others.

To further solidify your understanding, explain what you learned to someone else. Teaching is one of the most effective ways to reinforce learning and identify any gaps in your knowledge. It also disciplines the mind because you have to fully understand the subject to explain it.

Person You Taught:

____

Summary of What You Taught:

____

____

____

____

Intellectual Humility.

Aside from sharpening his critical thinking, one of the most important lessons John Stuart Mill learned from his father was intellectual humility. This principle kept him from seeking academic praise or viewing himself as intellectually superior.

Mill believed proper development of the mind was more important than natural intellectual ability. He spurned the idea of "brilliance" and instead believed that anyone could be trained to think well. With enough perseverance, individuals could even generate brilliant ideas on their own. This perspective was radical for its time and remains uncommon in modern educational approaches.

Mill also firmly believed that learning should be fun and engaging, but he distinguished this from only teaching easy and enjoyable subjects. He wanted to strike a balance between the harshness of his own education, which he found miserable, and the newer, more relaxed methods that seemed too easy on students.

While Mill's father's methods are not ideal, especially in the modern world, many of his strategies are very effective for fostering critical thinking so long as they are not applied so harshly. In-depth study, checks for understanding, engaged discussion, and physical movement all help improve critical thinking skills and memory. If one is a willing participant, they are helpful tools for shaping the mind.[36]

John Stuart Mill's *On Liberty*

---

[36] Elder, Linda. Cosgrove, Rush. (2007) John Stuart Mill: On Instruction, Intellectual Development, and Disciplined Learning. Foundation for Critical Thinking. https://www.criticalthinking.org/files/JohnStuartMill.pdf

Mill's moral philosophy is still as famous today as Kant's and contains many interesting ideas. His most well-known work, *On Liberty*, advances Mill's theory that people should be able to do whatever they wish as long as it doesn't hurt others.

This is more commonly known as the "harm principle," which aligns with the utilitarian philosophy endorsed by his father and mentors. For example, under this principle, someone should be free to choose a unique career path, like becoming a professional gamer or a freelance artist, as long as their choice doesn't negatively impact others.

Applying the harm principle to the concept of political freedom, Mill argued that individuals should be free to make their own choices without being controlled by the majority or falling victim to the "tyranny of the majority."

Instead of bending to the majority's will, a good government, according to Mill, would be one that promotes "the greatest good for the greatest number of people." He also recognized that a good government should balance the needs of the state with individual freedoms, and *On Liberty* explains the steps needed to find this balance.

For Mill, the primary role of the society's government is to serve the interests of the people. If it fails to do so, it becomes a form of tyranny, as the government's actions do not reflect the will of society at large. However, this ideal government relies on the assumption that people are aware of their own interests.

Another important idea of On Liberty was freedom of speech[37]. He argued that silencing a viewpoint harms not just the individual being censored but also deprives society of the opportunity to learn from and engage with that perspective.

Mill didn't care whether a viewpoint was right or wrong. He believed that if the opinion is correct, society loses the chance to correct errors with truth. If it is incorrect, society misses out on the valuable benefit of a clearer and more vivid understanding of truth achieved through its confrontation with error.

While Mill's emphasis on the importance of freedom of speech is compelling, this ideal faces significant challenges today.

It's important to think about how to handle people who knowingly spread false information. Mill valued debating all ideas, but he might not have fully considered the problem of those who lie or deceive. While discussing mistaken ideas can be helpful, it's unclear if the same benefits apply when dealing with people who deliberately spread falsehoods.

In his time, Mill didn't specifically address the problem of people who lie or deceive. However, he did think that hiding facts or twisting the truth should be criticized. He

[37] Alexander, N. (2023, October 26). *Reading John Stuart Mill's On Liberty in the Age of "Cancel Culture" and "Fake News"* Liberal Currents. https://www.liberalcurrents.com/reading-john-stuart-mills-on-liberty-in-the-age-of-cancel-culture-and-fake-news/

knew that people often act in what they think is good faith, making it tough to identify dishonesty.

Mill was worried that societal pressure could be even more restrictive than government rules when it comes to free speech. People were often silenced more by public opinion than by laws before. Today, even though we have more freedom to speak, some individuals still face issues if their views don't fit what's considered acceptable, sometimes unfairly.

When people are afraid to express their true thoughts, it impacts everyone. Mill believed that a thriving society needs a wide range of opinions and ideas. He thought people should be able to speak freely without fear, and that social pressure, not just government restrictions, is the biggest threat to free speech.

Mill also opposed the notion of a small group imposing beliefs on others. He argued that everyone should have the freedom to make their own cultural choices. By allowing individuals to pursue their own cultural and personal interests, society benefits from a diverse range of talents and perspectives, which contributes to its overall flourishing.

While these views might resemble those of John Locke, they differ in one crucial aspect: Mill did not believe in 'natural' rights as Locke did. Instead, he embraced Bentham's utilitarian philosophy of "the most good for the most people" and concluded that individual liberties created the most good for the most people in society.

Mill also agreed with Bentham that pain was never good, while pleasure was the ultimate aim. This is another classic precept of utilitarianism. Of course, this breaks down in big ways when we confront the idea of sacrifice and other such moral problems, but it's important to know this is in the background of Mill's other theories.

Mill argued that not all pleasures are the same. He made a distinction between higher pleasures (like intellectual and moral experiences) and lower pleasures (like drinking or dancing).

According to Mill, higher pleasures are more valuable because they offer deeper, more meaningful satisfaction. He believed that people who seek out and appreciate these higher pleasures would find a more profound and lasting happiness than those who only chase immediate sensory gratification.

This distinction remains relevant today, particularly in discussions about well-being and personal fulfillment. A recent study[38] support Mill's view, showing that people who engage in higher pleasures—such as cultural experiences, intellectual pursuits, or moral and ethical activities—report

---

[38] Fauzi, M. W. M., Hussein, N., Razali, M. Z. M., Anwar, N. A., & Omar, N. (2024). Intrinsic Motivation, Life Satisfaction and Happiness: Students at higher learning institution in Malaysia. In *Environment-Behaviour Proceedings Journal*. https://ebpj.e-iph.co.uk/index.php/EBProceedings/article/download/5767/3112

greater life satisfaction compared to those who focus mainly on lower pleasures.

Mill's notion that those who pursue higher pleasures contribute more significantly to societal good also finds resonance in modern contexts. Individuals who engage in intellectual and moral pursuits often contribute more profoundly to societal progress, innovation, and ethical standards. This aligns with Mill's view that personal development and societal advancement are interconnected. Those who seek higher pleasures are not only enhancing their own lives but also fostering a more enlightened and progressive society.[39]

Women's Rights.

Mill's beliefs led him to support many causes such as abolition, political equality, and most importantly, women's rights. He saw the subjugation of women as a huge barrier to society's progress, and therefore contrary to his utilitarian moral philosophy.

Women's inability to work in the professions, own property, have custody of their children, or divorce, blocked society from progressing in Mill's view. Besides, it was morally incorrect as no man would ever assume this sort of societal position of his own free will. If we look at it from a

---

[39] Philosimply. (2018) John Stuart Mill. Philosimply. http://www.philosimply.com/philosopher/mill-john-stuart

Kantian angle (as Mill did), it was not compatible with a moral society according to the categorical imperative.

Mill's treatise *On the Subjugation of Women* is his most famous feminist work, where he argues that women are not inherently inferior to men. He contended that women should be treated equally under the law. Addressing the common argument of his time—that women were naturally inferior and therefore needed to be dominated by their husbands—Mill countered that since women had never fully experienced freedom, we cannot know their true nature if they were given the same opportunities as men.

During his time as a Member of Parliament, Mill put his writings into practice to fight for women's suffrage and legal status. He also privately followed his own prescriptions, writing a sort of pre-nuptial agreement wherein he declared that he forfeited all his 'rights' as a husband over his wife as encoded in British legal statute.

Feminists like Mary Wollstonecraft had already published work about the rights of women before Mill wrote his feminist treatise, but he was the first man to practice what we now call "he for she" feminism. Though he had no direct personal stake in the game, he still championed women's causes in the intellectual world through his philosophy.

Think Like Mill.

Enhance your critical thinking abilities by applying John Stuart Mill's principles to various real-world scenarios and examining how they can guide your analysis and decision-making.

1. The online forum you are moderating is filled with heated debates, including some offensive comments. Will you restrict or remove offensive comments to prevent harm? Why?

____

____

____

____

____

2.You're at a company meeting where a new policy is being discussed to ensure equal pay and opportunities for women. Will you support this policy?

____

____

____

____

3. The government proposes a new initiative to track phone calls as a measure to enhance security and prevent crime. How do you think individual privacy should be balanced against these public safety concerns?

____

____

____

____

4. During a health crisis, the government has mandated vaccinations for everyone to protect public health. Do you support this mandate? How do you think individual freedoms should be weighed against the need for these public health measures?

5. As the curator of a public park displaying a piece of controversial art that has sparked mixed reactions from the community, you need to decidc whether to allow this art to remain on display. Should this controversial piece be permitted in public spaces? Why?

Chapter 7: William Graham Sumner

"[Students] educated in [critical thinking] cannot be stampeded by stump orators and are never deceived by dithyrambic oratory. They are slow to believe. They can hold things as possible or probable in all degrees, without certainty and without pain. They can wait for evidence and weigh evidence, uninfluenced by the emphasis or confidence with which assertions are made on one side or the other. They can resist appeals to their dearest prejudices and all kinds of cajolery. Education in the critical faculty is the only education of which it can be truly said that it makes good citizens."

William Graham Sumner, *Folkways*, (pp. 633-634).

Background.

William Graham Sumner was an American social scientist and scholar who was one of the key innovators of critical thinking in the 20th century, as well as one of the founders of the field of sociology.

Born in 1840 and educated at Yale, where he later became a professor, Sumner made significant contributions to the fields of sociology and anthropology, *Folkways*, is considered a landmark in the field as well as in the process of critical thinking. He recognized how the human brain's thinking is sociocentric by nature—meaning we're wired to think as social animals. He also realized that schools worked as centers of indoctrination rather than institutions designed to foster critical thinking.

Sumner believed that schools were designed to turn out the same sort of person, similarly to a cookie cutter. He saw this as a problem because if everyone is educated to think the same way, they can't challenge one another's ideas. He agreed with John Stuart Mill, whose views we've discussed earlier, that critical thinking was necessary for a quality education. Sumner also emphasized that teachers must be as informed as their students, upholding rigorous intellectual standards. He advocated for a teaching approach that valued precision and process, encouraging students to reach their own conclusions through critical examination.[40]

For Sumner, critical thinking involved interrogating one's positions to ensure they aligned with reality. He believed that critical thinking was a habit that could be developed, akin to Aristotelian principles, and that both men and women should have access to this training. Sumner believed that embracing critical thinking was essential for combating misinformation and maintaining societal order.

---

[40] Critical Thinking. (2018) Sumner's Definition of Critical Thinking. https://www.criticalthinking.org/pages/sumnerrsquos-definition-of-critical-thinking/412

Sumner's Vision of a Critical Society.

William Graham Sumner's *Folkways* tackled how social change unfolds through the lens of social history. He explored how everyday customs and social norms, what he dubbed "folkways," shape human behavior.

He also developed the theory of ethnocentrism, or the attitude of looking at the world from one's own cultural viewpoint. This rule applies to any culture, any race, any social group. Although this isn't necessarily xenophobia, it does entail a sense of cultural/ethnic superiority in relation to other groups. Sumner believed that this dark side of human nature could also be traced through the development of human society.

Sumner argued that social behavior evolves independently of government intervention, making political reform largely ineffective. Unlike figures such as Herbert Spencer, who embraced Social Darwinism, Sumner rejected this theory by his death. He believed societal development was cyclical rather than linear, dismissing "survival of the fittest" as unnecessary and harmful, contributing to destructive ideologies.[41]

Sumner advocated for gender equality, humane treatment of sex workers, and women's rights, while maintaining Victorian views on the family unit. His vision of

[41] Sumner, W. (1940). Folkways: A Study of the Sociological Importance of Usages, Manners, Customs, Mores, and Morals, New York: Ginn and Co.

a “critical society,” involved embedding critical thinking in everyday life. He believed that such a society, though theoretical, could prevent misconceptions and societal ills by fostering rational thought.

Despite human biases and emotions that hinder this ideal, Sumner emphasized that a robust educational system is crucial for nurturing independent and creative thinkers. This approach, he argued, is essential for addressing the complex challenges of the modern world.

How to Develop a Critical Society?

We know we’re capable of critical thinking—our history is full of remarkable achievements driven by human reason. Yet, as Sumner pointed out, honing our rational thinking isn’t automatic; it takes consistent effort. To work towards a critical society, we must continually strive to enhance our critical thinking abilities. A true critical society would involve individuals listening with open minds, setting aside personal biases, and assessing all viewpoints thoroughly.

Right now, the need for this kind of thinking couldn’t be clearer. Our planet is irrefutably suffering with dwindling resources and biomes, as well as the loss of countless lives due to extreme climates. Wars continue across the globe, often perpetuated by leaders upon their own people trying to warp reality itself by misinforming their citizens. Addressing these crises demands rigorous inquiry and collective effort.

Only by fostering reasoning and intelligence at a societal level can we hope to find pathways to peace and survival.

To develop this society, several steps need to be taken. Leaders must prioritize critical thinking as a vital skill for all members of society. Citizens need to think seriously about the problems within their society that can be fixed and figure out how to apply solutions. Without this collective effort, the society risks falling apart, divided by personal biases, flaws, and faulty thinking.

Pandemic Preparedness and Public Health Policy Exercise.

Imagine you're running for a seat in the Senate. One of the key issues your campaign will focus on is improving pandemic preparedness and public health policy. To succeed, you'll need to demonstrate not only your knowledge of the subject but also your commitment to critical thinking and evidence-based decision-making.

1. **Develop Your Platform:**

- **Research Task:** Spend time researching past pandemics, focusing on both the successes and failures in public health response. Pay particular attention to how different countries and states handled the COVID-19 pandemic.

Q1: Identify three critical weaknesses in the public health system exposed by the COVID-19 pandemic. How would you address these weaknesses if elected?

1.____

2.____

3.____

2. **Craft Your Policy:**

- **Policy Development Task:** Based on your research, develop a policy proposal that addresses these weaknesses. Consider the following:

How will you ensure equitable access to healthcare during a pandemic?

____

____

____

____

____

What measures will you put in place to improve communication between federal, state, and local health agencies?

How will you prioritize funding for public health infrastructure?

Q2: Draft a brief policy statement outlining your proposal.

3. **Communicate with the Public:**

- **Public Statement Task:** You're invited to speak at a town hall meeting. Prepare a short speech that explains your policy on pandemic preparedness and why it's crucial for public health. Focus on clarity and empathy to connect with voters.

Q3: Write your speech, emphasizing the importance of critical thinking and evidence-based policies in public health.

____

____

____

____

____

4. **Respond to Opposition:**

- **Debate Prep Task:** You'll face opposition from candidates who downplay the importance of pandemic preparedness or who believe in less government intervention. Prepare responses to potential criticisms of your policy, focusing on the benefits of proactive health measures.

Q4: Write down at least two key points to counter common arguments against pandemic preparedness.

____

____

____

____

5. **Build Community Support:**

- **Campaign Task:** To gain community support, you'll need to demonstrate how your policy will directly benefit your constituents. Create a campaign flyer or social media post that highlights the key aspects of your policy and invites the public to a virtual town hall.

Q5: Draft your flier or social media post. Make sure it's informative, engaging, and clear.

This activity is designed to help you think critically about public health policy and develop practical skills for public office. Your success in this campaign hinges on your ability to blend knowledge, critical thinking, and effective communication.

As we conclude this exploration into building a critical society, it's evident that moving from ideals to action is both necessary and challenging. The steps you've taken today offer practical insights for enhancing critical thinking within our communities. Remember, the journey to a critical society is not a straight path but a continuous effort requiring dedication and collective resolve.

The foundation of a critical society lies in a well-designed educational system that promotes free and open-minded thinking. John Stuart Mill, Sumner, and even Albert Einstein recognized the importance of nurturing independent thought to overcome societal flaws.

Einstein's experience with a rigid academic environment led him to understand that true creativity and intellectual growth often occur outside traditional boundaries. This underscores the need for an educational framework that fosters free thinking, perfectly aligning with the belief that critical thinking is the cornerstone of societal progress.

As you move forward, embrace the challenge of fostering a critical society. The insights from this activity, along with the principles we've discussed, can guide us toward meaningful progress. Together, let’s commit to nurturing critical thinking in every aspect of our lives, ensuring that our communities and workplaces are environments where thoughtful inquiry and open-mindedness thrive.

Chapter 8: Richard Paul and Linda Elder

Background.

Richard Paul and Linda Elder stand out as leading figures in the development of critical thinking until today. Richard Paul, a prominent philosopher and educator, began developing his theories on critical thinking in 1968, His Ph.D. dissertation at the University of California, Santa Barbara, laid the foundation for his extensive work.

By his passing in 2015, Paul had authored eight books and over 200 articles. He was the Director of Research and Professional Development at the Center for Critical Thinking in California; he was also the Chair of the National Council for Excellence in Critical Thinking. His methods for teaching critical thinking were influential across all age groups and educational levels, with lectures at prestigious institutions like Harvard University, the University of Chicago, and the University of Toronto. [42]

Linda Elder, Richard Paul's wife, began her career in psychology and is currently an educational psychologist, as well as the president of the Foundation for Critical Thinking and Executive Director of the Center for Critical Thinking. Her work focuses on critical thinking development and instruction.

---

[42] Dr. Richard Paul. http://www.criticalthinking.org/pages/dr-richard-paul/818

More specifically, she works on obstacles to developing critical thinking skills and how they relate to egocentric and socio-centric thought. These obstacles include ethnocentricity as a subset of sociocentrism, otherwise known as how group-relationships can adversely affect thought processes. Linda's research explores how thinking, feeling, motivation, and bias interplay, offering valuable insights into the relationship between thought and emotion.[43]

In 1980, Paul founded the Center for Critical Thinking at Sonoma State University in California, followed by the establishment of the Foundation in 1991 to support its work. The Center and the Foundation's output has been used in educational programs worldwide for developing critical thinking skills, including the Army Field Manual for officers in the military.

Paul believed critical thinking necessitated an understanding of thinking as a whole, fitting thinking into a paradigm, and ascertaining how thinking could be improved after these steps were taken. He saw critical thinking not only as a problem-solving tool but as a means to live a more fulfilled life, intertwining ethics with personal development. Thinking well was not just beneficial for the thinker; it was an act of service to the whole world.

The Paul-Elder Critical Thinking Model.[44]

---

[43] Dr. Linda Elder. https://www.criticalthinking.org/pages/dr-linda-elder/819

[44] Elder, L. and Paul, R. (2004). Adapted from The Thinker's Guide to the Art of Strategic Thinking: 25 Weeks to Better Thinking and Better Living.

Richard Paul's model for the development of critical thinking remains influential today and is arguably his most significant intellectual achievement. His model fuses theoretical standards of critical thinking with practical methods to develop in oneself and others. His model is composed of three main precepts, which we'll explore later:

1. **Elements of Thought**. The basic parts of reasoning.
2. **Intellectual Standards**. The criteria for evaluating the quality of reasoning.
3. **Intellectual Traits**. The qualities developed from consistently applying these standards to your thinking.

Paul and Elder published an extensive body of work detailing the evidence they found to support this model, addressing its application and potential challenges. According to the model, critical thinkers must regularly apply intellectual standards to the various elements of reasoning to cultivate important intellectual traits.

Elements of Thought.[45]

In 1997, Paul and Elder improved their model by providing two key aspects of good critical thinking: recognizing the elements of your thought process and being able to determine if you're using them correctly. Here is the detailed list of the individual elements:

[45] *Paul-Elder Critical Thinking Framework — University of Louisville Ideas To Action.* (n.d.). https://louisville.edu/ideastoaction/about/criticalthinking/framework

1. There is a **purpose** to all critical reasoning.

   Define your goal clearly, keep it separate from similar goals, regularly check your progress, and ensure it's both important and achievable.

2. The goal of critical reasoning is to resolve some **sort of intellectual issue**, whether that be a question, a problem, or a puzzle.

   Make sure you understand the question by saying it clearly, rephrasing it in different ways, breaking it into smaller questions, and figuring out if it has one right answer, depends on opinions, or needs different viewpoints.

3. All reasoning relies on **assumptions**.

   Recognize your assumptions and check if they make sense. Think about how these assumptions affect your perspective.

4. We all bring our **point of view** into our critical reasoning.

   Identify your own perspective, consider other viewpoints, and weigh their pros and cons. Strive to be fair and balanced in your evaluation.

5. We all base our reasoning on **data, information** and **evidence.**

   Base your claims on the available data and seek out both supporting and opposing information. Make sure all data is clear, accurate, relevant, and sufficient to address the issue.

6. All critical reasoning is filtered through **concepts and ideas**.

   Explain your main ideas simply, check if there are other ways to understand them, and make sure you use the right words carefully.

7. Critical reasoning always necessitates **interpretation** to reach a **conclusion**.

   Make conclusions only from the evidence you have and check if they match up. Also, identify any assumptions you used to reach these conclusions.

8. Critical reasoning always has **implications** or **consequences.**

   Look at both the good and bad outcomes of your reasoning and think about all possible results.

Evaluate Reasoning.

Apply the eight elements of thought to analyze others' work, specifically an article of your choice. This exercise will aid you in assessing the article's structure and reasoning.

Title of Chosen Article:

____

1. (Purpose) What is the purpose of the reasoner (author) in the article?

____

____

____

____

2. (Question) Is the main question at issue well-stated in the article?

____

____

____

____

3. (Information) Does the writer provide relevant evidence, experiences, or information necessary for the issue?

____

____

____

____

4. (Concepts) Are key concepts clarified when necessary?

5. (Assumption) What assumptions does the writer make?

6. (Inference) How does the writer develop their reasoning to arrive at their conclusions?

7. (Point of View) Does the writer consider alternative viewpoints or objections?

8. (Implications) What are the implications and consequences of the writer's position?

Universal Intellectual Standards.[46]

For Elder, effective reasoning hinges on nine key intellectual standards: clarity, accuracy, precision, relevance, depth, breadth, logic, significance, and fairness.

It's not possible for reasoning to be truly sound if it fails to meet these standards. If someone claims their reasoning is valid but admits it's unclear, inaccurate, imprecise, irrelevant, narrow, superficial, illogical, trivial, and unfair, that reasoning is fundamentally flawed. Embracing these standards is essential for developing strong, rational thinking and understanding their broader application.

1. **Clarity** means making sure your ideas are easy to understand. If something isn't clear, you can't tell if it's right or relevant.

   For example, instead of asking, "How can we improve health care?" which is too broad, you might ask, "What can be done to make sure everyone has access to affordable health care?"

2. **Accuracy** means making sure a statement is free from errors, mistakes, or distortions and correctly reflects the facts.

[46] Paul, R., & Elder, L. (2013). Critical Thinking: Intellectual Standards Essential to Reasoning Well within Every Domain of Human Thought, Part Two. *Journal of Developmental Education*, *37*(1), 32–33. http://files.eric.ed.gov/fulltext/EJ1067269.pdf

For example, saying "The Earth has three moons" is clear but not accurate. To ensure accuracy, you need to check if the statement aligns with reality.

3. **Precision** means specific and detailed. A statement can be clear and accurate but still imprecise, such as saying "The meeting starts in the afternoon" without specifying a time. Precision involves providing enough detail to make understanding clear.

4. **Relevance** means being directly related to and important for the matter at hand. For instance, a person might focus on the color of a car when discussing its safety features. While the color is clear and accurate, it's irrelevant to evaluating the car's safety.

5. **Depth** means understanding the complexities and multiple interrelationships within a situation, idea, or question. It involves a thorough examination of all relevant factors rather than just a superficial glance.

   For instance, saying "Exercise is good for health" is clear, accurate, precise, and relevant, but it lacks depth because it doesn't explore how different types of exercise impact various aspects of health.

6. **Breadth** means considering a range of perspectives and viewpoints, ensuring a comprehensive and open-minded approach to understanding a topic.

An example of breadth is considering multiple perspectives on healthcare reform, such as those from patients, providers, economists, and policymakers, rather than just one viewpoint.

7. **Logic** means that the different parts of your reasoning fit together without contradictions and adhere to principles of sound judgment and rationality.

   If you argue that eating more fruits and vegetables will improve your health and then claim that it has no impact on health, your reasoning is contradictory. Both statements can't be true at the same time.

8. **Significance** means focusing on what is most important or impactful. In reasoning, it's essential to prioritize substantial information and key ideas over trivial details.

   For instance, when discussing a business strategy, focusing on "What are the long-term goals for growth?" is more significant than just "What's the next quarterly report going to look like?"

9. **Fairness** means being free from bias, dishonesty, favoritism, or selfish interests. It requires considering all relevant viewpoints equally and objectively, without letting personal feelings or interests cloud judgment.

For example, when evaluating a job candidate, fairness means assessing each candidate based on their qualifications and skills rather than personal biases or favoritism.

Formulate Questions Based on Intellectual Standards.

Develop your ability to create questions that adhere to key intellectual standards. For each standard, use the given example to inspire a question that aligns with the standard.

1. In a meeting, someone asked, "What can be done about the education system in America?" However, the question is unclear. Formulate a question to achieve clarity.

____

____

____

____

2. An article claims, "The new policy will significantly reduce unemployment rates," but the evidence provided is outdated. Create a question to ensure the accuracy of the information.

____

____

____

____

3. A report states, "Many people are dissatisfied with the healthcare system," but does not specify which aspects or demographics are most affected. Formulate a question to increase precision.

____

____

____

____

4. During a discussion about environmental policies, someone brings up the benefits of a new technology unrelated to the policy in question. Develop a question to ensure relevance.

____

____

____

____

5. A debate on income inequality presents only basic statistics without addressing underlying causes or solutions. Create a question that explores the deeper issues.

____

____

____

____

6. An opinion piece discusses the benefits of online education but ignores potential drawbacks. Formulate a question that considers other perspectives.

7. A presentation argues that reducing taxes will improve public services without explaining the connection between the two. Develop a question to address the logical connection.

8. A study highlights minor benefits of a new diet plan without discussing its overall impact on health. Create a question that assesses the significance of the findings.

Intellectual Traits.[47]

Finally, here are the Intellectual Traits people can develop on their journey to becoming better critical thinkers:

[47] Paul, R., & Elder, L. (2008). The Miniature Guide to Critical Thinking Concepts & Tools. https://home.miracosta.edu/rfrench/documents/MiniGuidetoCT.pdf

1. **Intellectual humility** is about recognizing the limits of your knowledge. It means understanding that your views may be incomplete and that you're prone to biases.

   If you're discussing a controversial topic and someone presents new evidence, intellectual humility encourages you to consider their points rather than stubbornly sticking to your original stance. It's not about being weak—it's about rejecting arrogance and staying open to learning and revising your beliefs when needed.

2. **Intellectual courage** is about confronting ideas we strongly oppose and giving them a fair hearing, even when it's uncomfortable. It's recognizing that some beliefs we dismiss as absurd might actually have some truth, while those we've accepted may be misleading.

   For example, if everyone around you believes in a certain political ideology, it takes courage to explore opposing views and admit they might have valid points. This bravery is essential because it helps us stay true to our own thinking, even when it means challenging the beliefs of our social group.

3. **Intellectual Empathy** means actively putting yourself in others' shoes to genuinely understand their perspectives, while being aware of our natural tendency to see our own beliefs as the truth. It's

about accurately grasping others' viewpoints and reasoning, even when they differ from your own.

For example, if you once believed strongly in something but later realized you were wrong, empathy helps you recognize that you could be mistaken again, encouraging open-mindedness in the face of differing opinions.

4. **Intellectual Independence** is about having rational control over your beliefs, values, and conclusions. It means thinking independently and taking command of your thought processes. You analyze and evaluate beliefs based on reason and evidence, questioning when it's logical, believing when it's justified, and conforming only when it's rational to do so.

   For example, rather than just going along with popular opinion, intellectual autonomy drives you to form your own reasoned conclusions.

5. **Intellectual Integrity** involves being true to your own thinking and applying consistent intellectual standards. It means holding yourself to the same rigorous standards of evidence and proof that you expect from others, practicing what you advocate, and honestly admitting any inconsistencies in your own thoughts and actions.

For instance, if you expect others to provide solid evidence for their claims, intellectual integrity requires you to do the same with your own beliefs.

6. **Intellectual Perseverance** is the commitment to using insights and truths despite challenges, obstacles, or frustrations. It involves sticking to rational principles even when faced with irrational opposition and persisting through confusion and unsettled questions to achieve deeper understanding.

   For example, intellectual perseverance drives you to continue exploring a complex issue, even when the answers aren't immediately clear or when others discourage your efforts

7. **Confidence in Reason** is the belief that, in the long run, the best outcomes for oneself and humanity will come from encouraging rational thinking. It involves faith that, with the right support, people can develop their own rational faculties, form logical viewpoints, and persuade others through reason.

   For example, confidence in reason means trusting that open dialogue and logical debate will lead to better understanding, even when faced with deep-seated biases.

8. **Fairmindedness** is about treating all viewpoints equally, setting aside personal feelings, interests, or biases. It involves sticking to intellectual standards

impartially, without giving preference to your own or your group's perspective.

For example, fairmindedness means you should evaluate an opposing argument with the same rigor and openness as you would your own, even if it goes against your beliefs.

Practice Intellectual Traits.

For each trait, read the scenario and formulate a response to the question that demonstrates the application of the trait.

1. You've been insisting that the best way to save money on groceries is by buying in bulk. A friend shows you research indicating that buying only what you need reduces waste and can actually save money. To show **intellectual humility**, what would you do in response to the new evidence?

____

____

____

____

____

____

____

____

____

____

2. At a family gathering, everyone is excited about a new home renovation idea that you think is impractical and could be expensive. To show **intellectual courage**, how would you bring up your concerns and suggest alternative ideas without causing conflict?

____

____

____

____

____

____

____

____

____

____

3. You've always preferred working in a quiet office, but a colleague thrives in a noisy, collaborative environment. To show **intellectual empathy**, how would you understand and appreciate your colleague's preference for a noisy workspace?

____

____

____

____

____

____

____

____

4. Your social group widely supports a particular health fad diet. Instead of simply following the trend, you want to evaluate the diet on your own. To show **intellectual independence,** what steps would you take to evaluate this new workout trend?

5. You often critique friends for spreading unverified news on social media, but you recently shared an article with questionable sources. To show **intellectual integrity**, how would you address the issue with your own post and ensure your information is reliable?

6. You're learning a new language and find it challenging to grasp complex grammar rules. Despite feeling frustrated, you are determined to improve. To show **intellectual perseverance**, how would you continue your studies and overcome the difficulties you face?

7. During a debate about the benefits of electric cars, some people dismiss your well-reasoned arguments as idealistic. To show **confidence in reason,** how would you keep advocating for your position and trust that rational discussion will lead to better understanding?

8. Your neighborhood is debating whether to build a new park or a shopping center. You have a personal preference for the park, but you need to fairly consider the benefits of the shopping center as well. To show **fairmindedness**, how would you evaluate both sides of the debate impartially?

By using the elements of reason, asking questions based on intellectual standards, and applying key intellectual traits, you've really stepped up your critical thinking skills, thanks to the Paul-Elder model. This approach helps you analyze and evaluate information more effectively and understand complex issues more deeply. With these enhanced skills, you're better equipped to tackle challenges from different angles, make more informed decisions, and approach problems with greater clarity.

Conclusions

As we wrap up our exploration of critical thinking, we have traced its development from Socrates and Aristotle to Richard Paul and Linda Elder. Each thinker has contributed valuable insights about questioning, mental organization, education, practical applications, and self-examination.

Socrates taught us to ask the right questions and dig deeper to uncover the truth.

Aristotle showed the power of categorizing and structuring thoughts through deductive reasoning, organizing knowledge to make logical sense of the world.

Aquinas emphasized intellectual disputation, showing that examining different viewpoints enriches understanding.

Bacon championed empirical evidence, advocating for observation and experimentation over abstract reasoning.

Descartes introduced the value of doubt and skepticism, urging us to question accepted truths and seek clarity through reason

Kant bridged the gap between reason and empirical evidence, showing how our minds filter and interpret information.

Mill highlighted critical thinking as a teaching process, shaping education to foster independent thought.

Sumner pointed out our inherent biases and offered methods to overcome them for clearer thinking.

Paul and Elder provided practical tools for developing critical thinking skills, accessible to anyone regardless of their background.

These varied critical thinkers all convey a common message: critical thinking is a universal tool for navigating life. It's not reserved for scholars or elites but is accessible to everyone. We can all apply critical thinking in our daily lives. It enriches our experiences, sharpens our problem-solving skills, and makes us better global citizens.

You don't need to have a Ph.D. or be a member of the intelligentsia to be a critical thinker. It’s not about having certain political beliefs or fitting into a specific philosophical mold. You just need to be open to other people's ideas, and able to question your own preconceptions, ideas, and thought processes.

The most important quality of the critical thinker is being open to change, while having confidence in your quest for truth. If you work hard to develop your critical thinking skills, drawing on the wisdom of these great minds, you'll unlock your reasoning power and boost your confidence in your beliefs. You'll also find it easier to connect with others, even when they see things differently. These skills are invaluable in today's world, and the best part is, anyone can develop them. Keep practicing, and you'll soon see yourself becoming a sharp, effective critical thinker.

As I bid farewell, thank you for joining us on this intellectual journey. Wishing you all the best as you continue your quest for insight and understanding. Farewell, and stay curious!

Respectfully,
A. R.

Before You Go…

I would be so very grateful if you would take a few seconds and rate or review this book on Amazon. Reviews – testimonials of your experience - are critical to an author's livelihood. While reviews are surprisingly hard to come by, they provide the life blood for me being able to stay in business and dedicate myself to the thing I love the most, writing.

If this book helped, touched, or spoke to you in any way, please leave me a review and give me your honest feedback.

Thank you so much for reading this book!

About the Author

Albert Rutherford

Blind spots can affect our lives without us realizing it. We often try to address our problems, but we rely on incorrect assumptions, faulty analysis, and misguided deductions. This leads to confusion, stress, and annoyance in our personal and professional connections.

Instead of jumping to conclusions prematurely, we can learn to evaluate information correctly and consistently to make better decisions. Developing systems and critical thinking skills can help us collect and assess data, as well as create impactful solutions in any situation.

Albert Rutherford has dedicated his life to finding evidence-based practices for optimal decision-making. His mantra is to ask better questions, to find more accurate answers, and to draw profound insights. In his free time, Rutherford pursues his long-cherished dream of becoming an author. He enjoys spending time with his family, reading the latest science reports, fishing, and pretending to know about wine. He firmly believes in Benjamin Franklin's words, "An investment in knowledge always pays the best interest."

Read more books from Albert Rutherford:
Advanced Thinking Skills

The Systems Thinker Series
Game Theory Series
Critical Thinking Skills

Reference List

Academia. (2018) Francis Bacon's Four Idols. https://www.academia.edu/10388379/Using_Francis_Bacons_Idols_to_Foster_Critical_Thinking?auto=download

Alexander, N. (2023, October 26). Reading John Stuart Mill's On Liberty in the Age of "Cancel Culture" and "Fake News" Liberal Currents. https://www.liberalcurrents.com/reading-john-stuart-mills-on-liberty-in-the-age-of-cancel-culture-and-fake-news/

Aquinas, Thomas. (1981) Summa Theologica. Christian Classics.

Belkind, Ori. (2021). Bacon's Inductive Method and Material Form. 58. 57-68.

Boammaaruri. (2017) René Descartes on critical thinking and avoiding error in judgments. https://boammaaruri.blog/2017/05/15/rene-descartes-on-critical-thinking-and-avoiding-error-in-judgments/

Brook, Andrew, "Kant's View of the Mind and Consciousness of Self", *The Stanford Encyclopedia of Philosophy* (Winter 2018 Edition), Edward N. Zalta. https://plato.stanford.edu/archives/win2018/entries/kant-mind/

Careful Nursing. (2015) Critical Thinking: Guidelines from Thomas Aquinas. http://www.carefulnursing.ie/go/blog/2015-05/critical-thinking-guidelines-from-thomas-aquinas

Ciliberto, G.(2019, January 28) 4 Practices of Saint Thomas Aquinas that Influence Us Today . Dominican Sisters of Hope. https://ophope.org/spirituality/saint-thomas-aquinas-feast-day-dominican-order/ Sayles, N.(2013)

Critical Thinking. (2018) The Role of Socratic Questioning in Thinking, Teaching, and Learning. http://www.criticalthinking.org/pages/the-role-of-socratic-questioning-in-thinking-teaching-amp-learning/522

Critical Thinking. (2018) Sumner's Definition of Critical Thinking. https://www.criticalthinking.org/pages/sumnerrsquos-definition-of-critical-thinking/412

Custom Writing Tips. (2018) The Importance of Critical Thinking. Custom Writing Tips. https://customwritingtips.com/component/k2/item/9848-the-importance-of-critical-thinking.html?tmpl=component&print=1

das Neves, J.C., Melé, D. Managing Ethically Cultural Diversity: Learning from Thomas Aquinas. J Bus Ethics 116, 769–780 (2013). https://doi.org/10.1007/s10551-013-1820-1

Dika, Tarek R., "Descartes' Method", The Stanford Encyclopedia of Philosophy (Summer 2024 Edition), Edward N. Zalta & Uri Nodelman (eds.), https://plato.stanford.edu/archives/sum2024/entries/descartes-method/

Dobrijevic, D. (2021, December 17). *Geocentric model: The Earth-centered view of the universe.* Space.com. https://www.space.com/geocentric-model

Dr. Linda Elder. https://www.criticalthinking.org/pages/dr-linda-elder/819

Dr. Richard Paul. http://www.criticalthinking.org/pages/dr-richard-paul/818

Elder, Linda. Cosgrove, Rush. (2007) John Stuart Mill: On Instruction, Intellectual Development, and Disciplined Learning. Foundation for Critical Thinking. https://www.criticalthinking.org/files/JohnStuartMill.pdf

Elder, L. Paul, R. (2004). Adapted from The Thinker's Guide to the Art of Strategic Thinking: 25 Weeks to Better Thinking and Better Living.

Farnam Street. (2018) Francis Bacon and the Four Idols of the Mind. https://fs.blog/2016/05/francis-bacon-four-idols-mind/

Fauzi, M. W. M., Hussein, N., Razali, M. Z. M., Anwar, N. A., & Omar, N. (2024). Intrinsic Motivation, Life Satisfaction and Happiness: Students at higher learning institution in Malaysia. In *Environment-*

Behaviour Proceedings Journal. https://ebpj.e-iph.co.uk/index.php/EBProceedings/article/download/5767/3112

Frederick C. Beiser, (2002) German Idealism: The Struggle Against Subjectivism, 1781-1801, Harvard University Press.

Hart, Greg. (2015) The Passing of a Critical Thinking Giant: Richard Paul (1937–2015). https://www.skeptic.com/reading_room/richard-paul-tribute/

Kannadan, Ajesh (2018) "History of the Miasma Theory of Disease," ESSAI: Vol. 16 , Article 18. Available at: https://dc.cod.edu/essai/vol16/iss1/18

Kantian School. (2012) Immanuel Kant and Critical Thinking. http://kantianschool.blogspot.com/2012/02/immanuel-kant-and-critical-thinking.html

Kraut, Richard (2017). Socrates. Encyclopedia Britannica. Encyclopedia Britannica, Inc.

Krasue, P. (2019, July 19). Aquinas on free will, sin, and ethics. https://minervawisdom.com/2019/07/19/aquinas-on-free-will-sin-and-ethics/#_ftn2

Kwantlen Polytechnic University. (2018) Critical Thinking through Socratic Questioning. https://www.kpu.ca/sites/default/files/Learning%20Centres/Think_Critical_LA.pdf

Matthews, Professor Steven (2013). Theology and Science in the Thought of Francis Bacon. Ashgate Publishing, Ltd. ISBN 9781409480143.

Michael Frede, "Stoic vs. Peripatetic Syllogistic", Archive for the History of Philosophy 56, 1975, 99-124.

Paul-Elder Critical Thinking Framework — University of Louisville Ideas To Action. (n.d.). https://louisville.edu/ideastoaction/about/criticalthinking/framework

Paul, Richard. Elder, Linda. Bartell, Ted. (1997)A Brief History of the Idea of Critical Thinking. Critical Thinking. http://www.criticalthinking.org/pages/a-brief-history-of-the-idea-of-critical-thinking/408

Paul, R., & Elder, L. (2013). Critical Thinking: Intellectual Standards Essential to Reasoning Well within Every Domain of Human Thought, Part Two. Journal of Developmental Education, 37(1), 32–33. http://files.eric.ed.gov/fulltext/EJ1067269.pdf

Paul, R. and Elder, L. (1997). Socratic Teaching. Foundation For Critical Thinking. http://www.criticalthinking.org/pages/socratic-teaching/606

Paul, R., & Elder, L. (2008). The Miniature Guide to Critical Thinking Concepts & Tools. https://home.miracosta.edu/rfrench/documents/MiniGuidetoCT.pdf

Philosimply. (2018) John Stuart Mill. Philosimply. http://www.philosimply.com/philosopher/mill-john-stuart

Philosophy Basics. (2018) St. Thomas Aquinas. Philosophy Basics. https://www.philosophybasics.com/philosophers_aquinas.html

Ralph Raico (2018). Mises Institute, ed. "John Stuart Mill and the New Liberalism".

Research guides: France: Women in the Revolution: Marie Antoinette. (n.d.). https://guides.loc.gov/women-in-the-french-revolution/marie-antoinette

Shatz, I. (n.d.). Kant's categorical imperative: Act the way you want others to act. https://effectiviology.com/categorical-imperative/#How_to_use_the_categorical_imperative

Smith, Robin, "Aristotle's Logic", The Stanford Encyclopedia of Philosophy (Winter 2018 Edition), Edward N. Zalta. https://plato.stanford.edu/entries/aristotle-logic/#AriLogWorOrg

Stratton, Jon. (1999) Critical Thinking for College Students. Rowman & Littlefield Publishers. ISBN-10: 0847696022.

Sumner, W. (1940). Folkways: A Study of the Sociological Importance of Usages, Manners, Customs, Mores, and Morals, New York: Ginn and Co.

Thomson, J. (2022, April 19). Francis Bacon and the four barriers to truth. Big Think. https://bigthink.com/thinking/cognitive-bias-francis-bacon-idols/

Winter, T. (2017). Smarter thinking: The Socratic method. HPT by DTS. https://blog.hptbydts.com/smarter-thinking-the-socratic-method

Endnotes

[1] Kraut, Richard (2017). Socrates. Encyclopedia Britannica. Encyclopedia Britannica, Inc.

[2] Paul, Richard. Elder, Linda. Bartell, Ted. (1997)A Brief History of the Idea of Critical Thinking. Critical Thinking. http://www.criticalthinking.org/pages/a-brief-history-of-the-idea-of-critical-thinking/408

[3] Winter, T. (2017). Smarter thinking: The Socratic method. HPT by DTS. https://blog.hptbydts.com/smarter-thinking-the-socratic-method

[4] Paul, R. and Elder, L. (1997). Socratic Teaching. Foundation For Critical Thinking. http://www.criticalthinking.org/pages/socratic-teaching/606

[5] Kwantlen Polytechnic University. (2018) Critical Thinking through Socratic Questioning. https://www.kpu.ca/sites/default/files/Learning%20Centres/Think_Critical_LA.pdf

[6] Paul, R. (1993). Critical thinking: What Every Person Needs to Survive in a Rapidly Changing World. Sonoma State University, Center for Critical Thinking & Moral Critique. https://www.criticalthinking.org/data/pages/79/770a28b6dfcc0886bbeca1dd1195a2bf51363f3ba852e.pdf

[7] Critical Thinking. (2018) The Role of Socratic Questioning in Thinking, Teaching, and Learning. http://www.criticalthinking.org/pages/the-role-of-socratic-questioning-in-thinking-teaching-amp-learning/522

[8] Stratton, Jon. (1999) Critical Thinking for College Students. Rowman & Littlefield Publishers. ISBN-10: 0847696022.

[9]Smith, Robin, "Aristotle's Logic", The Stanford Encyclopedia of Philosophy (Winter 2018 Edition), Edward N. Zalta. https://plato.stanford.edu/entries/aristotle-logic/#AriLogWorOrg

[10]Michael Frede, "Stoic vs. Peripatetic Syllogistic", Archive for the History of Philosophy 56, 1975, 99-124.

[11]Scholasticism was a popular pedagogical school in medieval Europe rooted in the idea of disputation as a method for cultivating rigorous critical thought. It reached its height in Aquinas's era, which coincided with the development of the modern university as instructional institutions for the clergy.

[12]Philosophy Basics. (2018) St. Thomas Aquinas. Philosophy Basics. https://www.philosophybasics.com/philosophers_aquinas.html

[13]Ciliberto, G.(2019, January 28) 4 Practices of Saint Thomas Aquinas that Influence Us Today .Dominican Sisters of Hope. https://ophope.org/spirituality/saint-thomas-aquinas-feast-day-dominican-order/ Sayles,N.(2013)

[14]Careful Nursing. (2015) Critical Thinking: Guidelines from Thomas Aquinas. http://www.carefulnursing.ie/go/blog/2015-05/critical-thinking-guidelines-from-thomas-aquinas

[15] Krasue, P. (2019, July 19). Aquinas on free will, sin, and ethics. https://minervawisdom.com/2019/07/19/aquinas-on-free-will-sin-and-ethics/#_ftn2

[16]das Neves, J.C., Melé, D. Managing Ethically Cultural Diversity: Learning from Thomas Aquinas. J Bus Ethics 116, 769–780 (2013). https://doi.org/10.1007/s10551-013-1820-1

[17]Aquinas, Thomas. (1981) Summa Theologica. Christian Classics.

[18]Careful Nursing. (2015) Critical Thinking: Guidelines from Thomas Aquinas. http://www.carefulnursing.ie/go/blog/2015-05/critical-thinking-guidelines-from-thomas-aquinas

[19] Empiricism emphasizes observable evidence over logical reasoning and traditional thought, unless traditions are based on observed evidence. This is very different from Aristotle, who emphasized reasoning; instead, here real-life experience is the best teacher.

[20] Farnam Street. (2018) Francis Bacon and the Four Idols of the Mind. https://fs.blog/2016/05/francis-bacon-four-idols-mind/

[21] Kannadan, Ajesh (2018) "History of the Miasma Theory of Disease," ESSAI: Vol. 16 , Article 18. Available at: https://dc.cod.edu/essai/vol16/iss1/18

[22] *Research guides: France: Women in the Revolution: Marie Antoinette.* (n.d.). https://guides.loc.gov/women-in-the-french-revolution/marie-antoinette

[23] Dobrijevic, D. (2021, December 17). *Geocentric model: The Earth-centered view of the universe.* Space.com. https://www.space.com/geocentric-model

[24] Thomson, J. (2022, April 19). Francis Bacon and the four barriers to truth. Big Think.

https://bigthink.com/thinking/cognitive-bias-francis-bacon-idols/

[25] Belkind, Ori. (2021). Bacon's Inductive Method and Material Form. 58. 57-68.

[26] Matthews, Professor Steven (2013). Theology and Science in the Thought of Francis Bacon. Ashgate Publishing, Ltd. ISBN 9781409480143.

[27] Custom Writing Tips. (2018) The Importance of Critical Thinking. Custom Writing Tips. https://customwritingtips.com/component/k2/item/9848-the-importance-of-critical-thinking.html?tmpl=component&print=1

[28] Dika, Tarek R., "Descartes' Method", The Stanford Encyclopedia of Philosophy (Summer 2024 Edition), Edward N. Zalta & Uri Nodelman (eds.), https://plato.stanford.edu/archives/sum2024/entries/descartes-method/

[29] Boammaaruri. (2017) René Descartes on critical thinking and avoiding error in judgments. https://boammaaruri.blog/2017/05/15/rene-descartes-on-critical-thinking-and-avoiding-error-in-judgments/

[30] Frederick C. Beiser, (2002) German Idealism: The Struggle Against Subjectivism, 1781-1801, Harvard University Press.

[31]Kantian School. (2012) Immanuel Kant and Critical Thinking. http://kantianschool.blogspot.com/2012/02/immanuel-kant-and-critical-thinking.html

[32] Brook, Andrew, "Kant's View of the Mind and Consciousness of Self", *The Stanford Encyclopedia of*

Philosophy (Winter 2018 Edition), Edward N. Zalta. https://plato.stanford.edu/archives/win2018/entries/kant-mind/

[33] Shatz, I. (n.d.). *Kant's categorical imperative: Act the way you want others to act.* https://effectiviology.com/categorical-imperative/#How_to_use_the_categorical_imperative

[34] *Epistemology: A Priori vs. A posteriori; Analytic vs. Synthetic, Necessary vs. Contingent - Lucid Philosophy.* (2017b, September 14). Lucid Philosophy. https://lucidphilosophy.com/1019-2/

[35] Ralph Raico (2018). Mises Institute, ed. "John Stuart Mill and the New Liberalism".

[36] Elder, Linda. Cosgrove, Rush. (2007) John Stuart Mill: On Instruction, Intellectual Development, and Disciplined Learning. Foundation for Critical Thinking. https://www.criticalthinking.org/files/JohnStuartMill.pdf

[37] Alexander, N. (2023, October 26). *Reading John Stuart Mill's On Liberty in the Age of "Cancel Culture" and "Fake News"* Liberal Currents. https://www.liberalcurrents.com/reading-john-stuart-mills-on-liberty-in-the-age-of-cancel-culture-and-fake-news/

[38] Fauzi, M. W. M., Hussein, N., Razali, M. Z. M., Anwar, N. A., & Omar, N. (2024). Intrinsic Motivation, Life Satisfaction and Happiness: Students at higher learning institution in Malaysia. In *Environment-Behaviour Proceedings Journal.* https://ebpj.e-iph.co.uk/index.php/EBProceedings/article/download/5767/3112

[39] Philosimply. (2018) John Stuart Mill. Philosimply. http://www.philosimply.com/philosopher/mill-john-stuart

[40] Critical Thinking. (2018) Sumner's Definition of Critical Thinking. https://www.criticalthinking.org/pages/sumnerrsquos-definition-of-critical-thinking/412

[41] Sumner, W. (1940). Folkways: A Study of the Sociological Importance of Usages, Manners, Customs, Mores, and Morals, New York: Ginn and Co.

[42] Dr. Richard Paul. http://www.criticalthinking.org/pages/dr-richard-paul/818

[43] Dr. Linda Elder. https://www.criticalthinking.org/pages/dr-linda-elder/819

[44] Elder, L. and Paul, R. (2004). Adapted from The Thinker's Guide to the Art of Strategic Thinking: 25 Weeks to Better Thinking and Better Living.

[45] *Paul-Elder Critical Thinking Framework — University of Louisville Ideas To Action*. (n.d.). https://louisville.edu/ideastoaction/about/criticalthinking/framework

[46]Paul, R., & Elder, L. (2013). Critical Thinking: Intellectual Standards Essential to Reasoning Well within Every Domain of Human Thought, Part Two. *Journal of Developmental Education*, *37*(1), 32–33. http://files.eric.ed.gov/fulltext/EJ1067269.pdf

[47] Paul, R., & Elder, L. (2008). The Miniature Guide to Critical Thinking Concepts & Tools. https://home.miracosta.edu/rfrench/documents/MiniGuidetoCT.pdf

Made in the USA
Las Vegas, NV
07 December 2024

b5790215-c40a-45d3-a182-f36258c23f78R01